MANAGING EXTERNAL SUPPLIERS

CHANDOS BUSINESS GUIDES
PURCHASING AND PROCUREMENT

Chandos Business Guides are designed to provide managers with practical, down-to-earth information. The Chandos Business Guides are written by leading authors in their respective fields. If you would like to receive a full listing of current and forthcoming titles, please visit our web site www.chandospublishing.com or contact Melinda Taylor on email mtaylor@chandospublishing.com or direct telephone number +44 (0) 1865 882727.

New authors: we are always pleased to receive ideas for new titles; if you would like to write a Chandos Business Guide, please contact Dr Glyn Jones on email gjones@chandospublishing.com or direct telephone number +44 (0) 1865 884447.

Bulk orders: some organisations buy a number of copies of our books. If you are interested in doing this, we would be pleased to discuss a discount. Please contact Dr Glyn Jones on email gjones@chandospublishing.com or direct telephone number +44 (0) 1865 884447.

MANAGING EXTERNAL SUPPLIERS

BRIAN HUGHES

Chandos Publishing
Oxford · England

Chandos Publishing (Oxford) Limited
Chandos House
5 & 6 Steadys Lane
Stanton Harcourt
Oxford OX8 1RL
England
Tel: +44 (0) 1865 882727 Fax: +44 (0) 1865 884448
Email: sales@chandospublishing.com
www.chandospublishing.com

••

First published in Great Britain in 2001

ISBN 1 902375 79 3

Typeset by Concerto
Printed by Biddles, Guildford, UK

Contents

About the author

Brian Hughes graduated from Clare College, Cambridge, in 1962 with a Geography degree and, wishing to be measured and challenged in the commercial world, worked in the food industry for leading blue-chip companies.

He began as a management trainee at family-run J. Sainsbury and learnt the art of wielding (subtle and unspoken) power. Looking for a greater challenge, he moved back through the supply chain into tougher and more demanding appointments in the manufacturing sector. He directed the buying operations for Kraft Foods, United Biscuits and Dairy Crest. Brian believes that building a new purchasing and supply chain management team at Dairy Crest, creating internal confidence and respect, was his most rewarding corporate assignment.

Brian's consultancy practice, Hughes Associates, was founded in 1994 and supports assignments in many varied disparate sectors including government offices. It has established a valued reputation for innovative solutions and was the only small practice to be short-listed for the Kelly's Award for Excellence in Purchasing & Supply (1999).

The cross-fertilisation between the public and private sectors, when discussing mutual problems, has contributed considerable fun and arguments as differing purchasing philosophies meet and resulted in significant client benefits.

Having experienced the invaluable strength of support afforded by suppliers he became a firm disciple for partnerships. Working within multinationals provided an insight into the attitudinal differences between purchasing functions and their internal colleagues.

He continues to write, lecture and review with enthusiasm for a discipline that he believes is poorly rewarded. He hopes that this contribution will provoke lively discussion and debate.

The author can be contacted via the publishers.

CHAPTER 1

Rationale

The beginning

The purchasing function is responsible for defining the relationship with outside supplying companies. Buyers have the privilege of determining the character of the business interface and other functions will take their lead from this example. Their attitudes will reflect the company they represent and influence the supplier's responses. In many instances the buying staff perform a reverse role as salesmen in persuading, encouraging, cajoling and managing the business links.

In the determined effort to achieve any commercial advantage, buying styles will range from outright confrontation to full collaboration. Their influence cannot be overstated and, mishandled, may cause strong negative reactions; for example, begrudging compliance in times of plenty may, instantly, turn to revenge in times of shortage! It is always possible to achieve equable relationships while simultaneously constructing a competitive supply arrangement. While this is rarely easy, the advantages to be obtained will reflect the total commitment of both parties.

Suppliers form the greatest resource, freely available but often untapped and ignored. Beyond the familiar mantra of price, quality and service exist opportunities to use the talents of the supplying companies. To derive maximum value requires skill in constructing and developing the business relationships. In serving customers most companies will 'walk one more mile' so that their existing trading relationship is protected and, hopefully, enhanced. Salesmen will strive for customer satisfaction and may arrange work that, strictly, is peripheral to the direct cost of goods and services that they provide but is of considerable extra value to their customer. Fierce market competition prompts these 'outside' activities that, judiciously used, will deliver commercial advantages.

Most buyers understand the innate advantage of sharing problems and finding solutions together. The extent to which customers may benefit will vary widely; any abuse – betrayal of confidence – will raise serious misgivings from the supplier and shut off this flow of informal support.

The popular measure of buying performance is deduced by comparing actual costs against forecasts and the contribution to corporate profitability. It is simplistic and rudimentary. The ultimate value, however, of skilled buying is in obtaining terms significantly better than their company size would justify and which, frequently, is achieved by harnessing the resources of their suppliers.

This book, while recognising the pre-eminence of price, describes strategies that encompass a panoply of other factors involved in reaching company objectives.

Gaining sponsorship

Buying remains a Cinderella career that reflects general management uncertainty and, possibly, disinterest. In part this derives from the constant trumpeting of the expensive failures of the purchasing function.

Media articles defining these inefficiencies are pervasive and encourage the haunted look of practitioners. In 1996 British manufacturers were accused of squandering £2.4 billion a year through a lack of (objective) measurement and a failure to exploit opportunities in supply chain integration (A.T. Kearney & Manchester School of Management). It is small wonder that the function labours with poor imagery. Purchasing remains the province of masochists!

Its status is weak and the impact on company profitability imperfectly understood – except when the corporate trading period nears conclusion and the ensuing frantic scramble to achieve budgeted targets becomes overwhelming. Under these circumstances, suppliers become Aunt Sallys providing succour and rescue; knee-jerk reactions trigger buyers into furiously pummelling them into a hoped-for state of cost submission. It is an unedifying spectacle.

It is, therefore, an unassailable objective to gain the highest executive support possible; sponsorship from the chief executive (CEO) provides a protective shield that encourages widespread assistance and grants time for the commercial benefits to emerge.

Changing the internal perceptions will entail decommissioning many past practices and persuading managers that it is better to reach targets together, through a process of collaboration that supplants internal dissatisfaction with approbation! Supply chain coordination becomes a beacon of hope.

Modern enlightened management is bringing welcome changes by embracing schemes that mimic the early JIT (just-in-time) initiatives and rely extensively upon coordinated activities between supplier and customer. Proponents of this trading methodology have lauded the extraordinary savings realised, especially those near-instant cost benefits that result from the massive reduction in stockholding values! Sufficient universal acclaim, through profit improvements, has welcomed supply chain strategies and partnerships.

Implicit within this theatre is the inter-company linkage that we are to examine. Managing external suppliers is an exercise in perceptive and careful negotiation towards mutual benefits that transcend the old-fashioned confrontational stance. Often, achievement exceeds expectations so that the architects deliver considerable further advantages for their company. It is a competitive operating advantage indeed.

Justifying strong links with suppliers

Modern business is increasingly interdependent and each company or link within the supply chain has greater sensitivity to their supplier base than ever. Lean corporate structures, more detailed specifications for goods and services and the fashion for outsourcing non-critical functions characterise these changes. While customer imperatives remain the dominant driving force, reliance upon suppliers has increased dramatically.

In purchasing non-standard materials and services, either by their nature or the absence of ready alternative suppliers, the dependency becomes very important. Monopoly suppliers present great challenges in seeking collaborative balance. It is, perversely, such situations that can demonstrate the maximum benefits in supply chain coordination.

Every business seeks to reach lowest-cost manufacturing status as the most secure basis for continuing to trade profitably. Lean internal staffing structures, computerised support systems and the removal of repetitive quality checking procedures facilitate the aim to minimise overhead costs.

In the drive to reduce cost from every facet of company activity, the relationship with suppliers assumes paramount importance. While effective buying departments continuously review existing specifications and sourcing options for alternative materials, the assault on supply logistics costs has provided outstanding benefits that feed directly into profits, especially the early 'one-off' cash flow gains consequent upon decimating stock levels. Amazing operating savings ensue from the provision of forecasts to suppliers, with the 'extended' ownership of stocks being invoiced at the point of consumption.

The many variants on just-in-time have signally improved corporate profitability. In Britain it followed upon the brutal breaking of union power by Margaret Thatcher. *Quiescent labour is, therefore, critical to the future well being of lean supply arrangements*; recent industrial unrest has illustrated the potential damage that strike action may cause. Companies should have emergency procedures that anticipate disruptions.

Providing customers with least-cost offerings penalises market competitors with a heavy disadvantage that, hopefully, may prove to be terminal. Maximum price competition philosophy is a vibrant proponent of many successful multinationals, e.g. Wal-Mart. No company has the comfort of ignoring this economic tenet.

Selecting suppliers

Every company possesses a polymorphic portfolio of suppliers, each performing specific functions, often unique, so that relationships are different, always individual, and deserving of careful consideration.

Of serious import is the perceived dependency that the company has upon the supplier. This dependency will vary and most companies will possess their own evaluation and risk assessment. It will identify those key suppliers with whom special arrangements should be made and nurtured. This study concentrates on those relationships that develop and provide value beyond meeting the basic requirements.

Suppliers providing market standard goods and services will experience a priority weighting upon costs. It is the single factor of differentiation and characterises markets with low entry costs, simple production processes and many potential suppliers. Take the supply of cardboard boxes, for instance. The list of alternative suppliers is voluminous, the sector easily infiltrated and points of differentiation almost nil. The specification will match market levels and the dependency value is low; therefore, price becomes the sole discussion. It is very likely that such products suffer the threat of rejection and there is easy replacement for any unacceptable deliveries. There is little or no strain imposed upon the purchaser in this replacement scenario. It is unlikely that these materials would repay the effort of close attention except when the rejection rates become burdensome upon receiving sites.

When the goods and services are important, there is value in developing a separate strategy for each purchased item. Dependency encourages respect and focus; all supply chains have potent value to be extracted through collaborative examination. In these circumstances every component should be reviewed. Nothing is sacrosanct.

As dependency increases, this becomes more important. It is a factor in supplier selection (see Chapter 3), a process coordinated by purchasing, that relies heavily upon the knowledge and attitudes of other involved internal functions.

Relationship characteristics

The most contentious element of any relationship is the alignment of corporate objectives and the building of similar mind-sets. The relationship is a marriage and demonstrates the same characteristics; shared visions make collaboration easy. Anticipation and understanding of customer objectives eases difficult instances when the supplier is requested to 'perform beyond the definition of the agreement' and contribute a unique or atypical service.

It is natural to expect customer pre-eminence to dominate the contact attitudes but, while this may be understandable, the most productive arrangement establishes a balanced situation in which the supplier is empowered to disagree, argue and refine any suggestions provided by their client. Cross-fertilisation of ideas, proactive challenge and positive stress push the collaboration forward beyond most competitors and contributes to a very healthy scenario identified by improved performance and profitability.

Sycophantic praise does nothing for the business and, while sensitive handling is crucial, challenges seeking improvements are essential building blocks in achieving progress.

In times of trouble

In contrast attention should be given to any potential hazard that prevents the development of the relationship and which, inevitably, triggers separation and divorce. Caution is essential. Withdrawing from any relationship is very sensitive and special circumstances must be adequately protected as the privileged knowledge and shared access are unwound. Realisation will emerge slowly so that both parties may anticipate the final closure. The protection of special projects and their preservation is important. Consideration is essential (see Chapter 18). Too many companies have discovered, to their cost, how leaked disclosure of product information presaged commercial disaster.

How the game is played

Most business links involve several different functions other than purchasing, and direct contacts develop naturally. For example, quality control and logistics managers will communicate regularly so that, when a contract has been concluded, buying will be expected to maintain a watching brief to ensure a smooth and untroubled progression. It is, however, important to recognise that purchasing should manage the interface positively. Purchasing, having selected the supplier, will be responsible for ensuring that relationships function properly, problems will be resolved, discord removed and the dialogue managed to obtain maximum benefit. This may be a difficult and onerous task; it is for purchasing to direct activities. Creating a favourable ambience is critical.

Every activity has a cost value that impacts upon the viability of any business relationship and the aggregate costs represent the corporate overheads. If, for example, the supplier possesses an expensive marketing department to extend their product range beyond the basic materials supplied to the customer, it is logical that this element should be excluded from the product costs. As linking the businesses closer proceeds, the more such situations will need resolution; obviously successful suppliers are to be encouraged and supported but never at the expense of the ongoing business.

Shared control of the flow of stock from supplier to the customer's internal processes forms the earliest, and easiest, activity from which both companies experience massive benefits. As firm and projected forecasts of requirements are transferred, so the benefits should allow both companies to sense the enormous savings available and to fully comprehend the penal costs that follow irresponsible and erratic demand changes. Consigned to the wastepaper basket are these on-off forecasts that flow from the ultimate consumers as the client company assumes responsibility for 'smoothing' the volume flows. In spite of applying a short timescale, it delivers improved production management for your supplier. Most arrangements include a real commitment for a short-term period that creates certainty and confidence. Beyond this period the forecasts have an agreed variation (10%) within which both parties can operate.

The periods will vary depending upon the industry but this extension of stock management results in freeing up storage space. The immediate benefit is the single cash flow improvement but, as the operation becomes slicker, further incremental gains will be created. The most obvious improvement is removing the traditional fail-safe stocks held against the customer's change in forecast – inevitably late with an ability to disrupt production schedules and without the option of recovering these additional costs.

In constructing the operating systems, because of the impact on stocking levels, considerable attention is given to the accuracy, or otherwise, of the forecasts. This welcome focus emphasises the most difficult corporate activity. Forecasting customer requirements remains fraught and often subjective; inaccurate forecasting jeopardises the considerable gains to be derived from stock management systems. As matters improve, customers are demanding a share in the cost benefits in exchange for their forecasts and commitment. Sharing the cost savings has become a norm. You have to discuss the timescale provided for the supplier: short-term commitments, a mid-term forecast liable to variation and long-term forecasts for budgetary purposes.

Stock management systems need a clear definition of legal ownership as the arrangements become sophisticated. The provision of forecasts is the first step and, subject to a satisfactory installation, *encourages the subsequent acceptance of all stocks short of the production lines remaining the responsibility of the supplier* – both in a quality control and financial sense! The management of these stocks illustrates that ownership continues until you have need of their use in producing your products. This requires clarity concerning their ownership, especially when they are stored upon your manufacturing sites. The transfer of ownership is critical in assisting your reduction of staffing levels; gone are the internal quality control personnel checking that deliveries meet the agreed specifications.

Downside prospects are obvious but that which involves unofficial strike actions are most damaging. Swedish car manufacturer Volvo was surprised by a 1999 rogue strike at a key supplier; consequent upon this action Volvo advised all other suppliers that they were *not* liable for the results of such activities. It is naive to believe that union activities, whether unofficial or not, will not feature on the industrial landscape!

Anticipation of these eventualities is admirable and necessary; stocking levels at the sites, alternative sources of supply and, allied to the stock levels, the payment arrangement must all be considered. The last option is available wherever space is not a consideration and a delayed payment agreement could provide an attractive alternative solution.

Independent referees

Shock waves may follow the selection of suppliers made by the purchasing function as other functions react to a choice that they cannot support! Modern procedures, however, concentrate on building collective confidence and discussing the supply options before the final decisions are made. Removing concerns produces a positive response and allows the direct contact functions, production and distribution, to express their opinions and share responsibility for the ultimate choice.

It is natural to extend this shared experience into the evaluation programmes to ensure that the supplier continues to meet your expectations, both historical and present. Evaluation programmes are well developed and, in some instances, extremely detailed. It is a common mistake to create an extensive measurement programme beyond the basic essentials at the beginning.

A supplier evaluation programme facilitates the continuing pressure for improved performance as the measured factors increase. The programme will show the relative progress of each supplier so that those 'falling behind' are publicly identified. It is, therefore, an excellent tool to press the partnership into keeping abreast of competition.

The programme should contain factors that all functions value, for example the production will be keenly interested in material meeting company specifications and the timing of the delivery, both of which are essential to the efficient operation of production units. The supplier should agree the level of performance that is required to satisfy the client company. As the target is reached, a revised objective should be agreed to encourage continuous improvement.

Conversely any deterioration in performance provides the purchasing personnel with several options: reduction in business, termination of business and/or reduced pricing as a penalty measure. Such programmes are a valued negotiating opportunity and always provide the 'better' suppliers with an independent justification for increased business! Every business should incorporate these programmes into the relationship.

It is difficult to support many ultra-complex schemes that include a multitude of measures, in part because of the considerable time required for the collection, collation and analysis and, in part, the most effective schemes concentrate on achieving basic performance levels. These may be changed; variation attracts attention, as management alters the balance between activity priorities. All programmes should be electronically based to minimise manpower costs; many companies view this programme as needing additional resources.

Regular reviews should allow other functions to participate in sourcing considerations. It is a very useful tactic to employ if supplier rationalisation is deemed appropriate and other functions need to be involved in the preliminary discussions. Setting existing suppliers into an evaluation process enables selection to proceed with universal support. It is critical that these measures are constantly yielding positive information for supplier and customer. They should be ditched if this proves otherwise. Do not use management time to perform repetitive tasks lacking credibility.

Transferred responsibilities

Given the current practice of using internal quality control staff to check deliveries of purchased goods and services that rarely involves a complete assessment, there should be little logical objection to transferring this function to your selected supplier. It is not unreasonable to expect the materials, when they are presented to the end of any production line, to comply with the agreed specification. In consequence, the client company may continue to perform effectively with minimal stock-holding managed by the supplier. The customer determines the payment, on an agreed regular basis, as the usage is recorded for the presentation of the invoices. Staff levels continue to diminish and this arrangement facilitates the removal of a semi-efficient activity into an arrangement in which the supplier becomes formally liable for any production mishaps that are a direct consequence of out-of-specification materials being submitted. Packaging is a frequent miscreant and processing machinery may be extremely sensitive to variations, sometimes beyond any specification, quality control linkage and shared responsibilities. Historically, internal quality control systems do not provide comprehensive assurance for all delivered materials, especially packaging, so that obtaining the supplier's validation of packaging materials may be suspect. Packaging variations traditionally cause production problems.

Administration procedures

Reducing the paper trail to the minimum acceptable level should be obsessive. In collaboration with finance and audit managers, the opportunity to remove unnecessary and duplicated documentation provides amazing benefits. Often the use of independent advisers will encourage efficient streamlining that extends across the companies. The provision of electronic systems challenges hard-copy retention and signature requirements, and destroys inbuilt costs; it removes paper, mechanistic workloads and process delays and creates constructive time. Costs associated with purchase order processing are dramatically reduced; the savings support full integration of electronic systems between companies and dismiss the traditional administrative drudgery and frustration.

The introduction of these systems enables companies to extend their supplier base, perhaps even beyond that envisaged by rationalisation proponents. The costs for installing electronic systems have become so low that most supply companies can become potential partners without creating burdensome additional administration.

Payment arrangements have caused considerable resentment for suppliers, especially the smaller companies for whom your business represents vital throughput. Every invoice carries the statement of payment terms that, in most cases, are ignored by the customer. Any independent research exposes the sometimes considerable delay for payment. While this is recognised by all, including the UK government, attempting to rectify the apparent anomaly by law will fail. The unspoken balance of power militates against any formal constraint and the most appropriate arrangement is for the customer and supplier to reach an agreed basis for payment. Earlier payment than historical practice may yield additional financial gains for the customer, and the supplier will be grateful for certainty of payment. The alternative methods for credit transfer will provide fertile discussions, e.g. TT (telegraphic transfer) processing. Agreements should be formally confirmed so that invoices showing other terms do not confer legal precedent. Pragmatism has enabled the apparent discrepancy in payments not to disrupt relationships and efforts should be made to ignore any formal attempt to impose late payment penalties, especially between companies that have a long-standing relationship.

CHAPTER 2

Company strategies and the role of purchasing

Introduction

Companies construct a business plan, strategy or objective for the future. It has multiple threads encompassing most functions and describes the development and progress towards the aspirations on a defined timescale.

Many elements of the company strategy depend upon extraneous factors, including inflation, for which purchasing will have valued input. Forecasting price changes and competitor activity will gain from a purchasing observation. Too often marketing have assumed an unchanged pricing scenario and been surprised and disappointed when market circumstances generate major changes of which purchasing may have been aware and the internal information channel has broken down.

Irrespective of the perceived importance of purchasing it is critical that the function aligns its own ambitions with that of the company. Purchasing should define their objectives for approval; no functional unit can operate within a vacuum. A presentation of the goals should remove misunderstandings, refine expectations and raise the profile. Purchasing may have been viewed as a reactive group, only responding to internal requests for goods and services and having no proactive role. The strategy statement will crystallize that part of the corporate plan performed by purchasing. It educates new employees and reminds the company of its essential collaborative nature (see Chapter 5). The purchasing department cannot be viewed as isolated functionaries doomed to live their corporate life out in a caravan alongside the company car park!

A cautionary observation

Purchasing is a two-way activity, being the 'enabling' function between the client company and its suppliers. It faces both ways so that, while suppliers are an essential element, the internal relationships are equally critical. Unless purchasing has a confident understanding with several key company functions, energy will be dissipated and misspent.

Operational efficiency is dependent upon accurate statements of need, volumes, timescale and price levels on a lead-time basis that excludes any element of panic activity, whether purchasing additional volumes, finding a 'home' for unwanted materials, or altering supplier production schedules. Uncertainty brings the probability of extra costs. It is, however, true that variation is a constant and purchasing tactics must allow for this in several different approaches to their suppliers. Performing miracles, with or without the support of suppliers, must not 'blind' the company to the expectation that this is the activity norm. Purchasing need to continually persuade their company that costs, often hidden, surely follow inaccurate needs and their avoidance is achieved by excellent communication, understanding based on close relationships with the suppliers and the knowledge that most costs can be avoided by thoughtful planning.

Purchasing represents the suppliers during all internal debates and discussions. The role is very important and may require the presence of specific suppliers. The design and development of new products, solving costly logistical or process problems and examining many business options call for close discussion and exchange of information. Suppliers should be seen as additional eyes and ears in discovering market news; they have considerable access to many markets beyond the scope of many customers and are capable of maintaining an invaluable commentary.

Your internal customers will have a simple direct and uncompromising attitude to the functional achievements. Pay prices above those of your competitors and seek another job as soon as possible; beyond the plethora of additional factors within the buying remit is the unchanging objective of contributing lowest prices! Of course, there are other significant factors (see below) but the commercial ability to command premium prices is granted to a small Olympian elite. This focus provides the opportunity of declaring, openly, the purchasing performance measured in the chosen manner to advise internal customers. The analysis should, wherever possible, include market details concerning competitor activities. In most commercial ventures the position of competitors is vital. Creating regular reports for customers is very powerful and is recommended.

Extending options for internal customers

Buyers do, surprisingly, raise their heads from the war of attrition waged against the suppliers and seek, exhaustively, every supply option that provides commercial benefit for their internal customers. They will challenge every current specification with the objective of constructing a value table that details the balance between quality and price for other company functions. It allows marketing and production to build an assessment process from which they may judge the impact upon sales levels and production efficiencies. In some cases they may suggest raising specifications to achieve operational benefits, lower wastage and improved machine performance, and exchange that advantage with a higher unit price for the products received. This decision will always require the confirmation of the ultimate internal customer.

Their natural function is to seek 'lower' specifications if the suggested quality has, previously, been tried and accepted. There is no justification for using more expensive material unless the ultimate internal customer supports the practice. Unquestioning, undemanding buyers will consign their company to the business scrap heap.

Regular review forums are the essence of this situation. Ill-defined and undisciplined projects cause damage; small project groups formed and reformed at regular intervals should keep the business 'on its toes' and alert to alternative options. Buying is pivotal but needs the assistance of technical, production and marketing staff. Persuading internal customers is the key.

Purchasing is a corridor to the outside world! The awesome information flow that buyers receive, formally and informally, is invaluable. If the dissemination is properly managed, the company will benefit. Market information and details of competitor activity provided by suppliers are rich sources. Technical innovation, pricing changes, new products and companies, legislation, industrial actions and changes to manufacturing profiles may yield positive results.

These essential building blocks come freely from salesmen because they are either attempting to 'trade off' this service for an advantage to themselves or the relationship may be sufficiently convivial and interdependent that it is a natural element. Buyers are privileged to receive this information and are obliged to assess its value; in the modern world of information overload there is much dross.

Devolved ordering

Considerable analysis has emphasised the desire to segregate the purchasing of low-value items from the order procedure. Obvious examples are stationery and engineering spares; the repetitive nature of supply is such that any level of automation that could be introduced into the ordering procedures would be advantageous. Many companies have negotiated an overall contract, priced by each separate product, against which internal sections may order without any further involvement from their purchasing colleagues. The process has sufficient details to facilitate the complete administrative cycle, from order and delivery to invoice payment.

Purchasing is responsible for the prior negotiations, perhaps with more than one supplier so that the internal customer has freedom of choice, and the internal customer manages the stock levels and payment approval. There are various systems, e.g. purchasing cards that provide analysis of expenditure that facilitates control. The advantage is to give some self-determination to the internal sections; it has valuable psychological benefits.

Supplier development programmes

The objective of a supplier development programme is to encourage key suppliers to improve their economic production basis. Sometimes this will require technical support, financial assistance or blind insensitive pressure so that the competitive edge is honed. These programmes embrace a multitude of activities that are studied elsewhere but the important premise is to concentrate on those processes that directly impact on the service provided. It is an easy delusion to provide assistance for a wide range of activities that extend beyond the brief so that the original objective becomes lost!

Building firewalls against competitors

Monogamy is difficult but wedding your company to a small number of suppliers contains similar challenges. If the relationship includes shared information of special significance to one partner then market relationships involving the other partner may be important. The risk of sensitive information becoming known by a direct competitor is of material concern. In a world where every buyer and salesman indulges in discovering business information about the direct competition nothing is foolproof, but it is important that maximum protection be obtained.

Understanding the pre-eminence of your position at the supplier gives some indication as to the extent to which you may 'demand' protection. It will be obvious that key customers are likely to have their wishes respected. It is probable that suppliers will not be servicing competing 'giants' for exactly the same motivation. It would be impossible to separate the customer's interests and could, potentially, damage your business.

Investment

Companies may be faced with 'make or buy' decisions as they design and develop new products. Such situations could include the option of joint ventures or providing an existing supplier with sufficient commercial support that they would construct a supply arrangement. The customer may have constraints on available cash or perceive a 'better' use for their resources and need to persuade a supplier of the attractiveness in supplying their need. Firm contractual statements may unlock the logjam and allow the construction to proceed.

When the required product is innovative, the supplier will demand unequivocal evidence of support to recover any losses in the event of product failure. The discussions will include purchasing, although the final decision may be exercised by another function. Committing company monies for long-term contractual agreements will need higher sanction.

Supplier rationalisation

Reducing supplier numbers automatically transfers increased business to the remaining suppliers. The rationalisation process should be accompanied by a price reduction that stretches into the future. There are innumerable positive logistics benefits – fewer deliveries, less administration, etc. – but the greater commitment implies better pricing. There is no standard format for measuring success but forecasted savings must preface the rationalisation project. These benefits may be delivered in different guises – often reflecting the importance of each supplier! Those who are 'secondary' may be encouraged to offer (a) terms in advance of the trading period or (b) regular backdated rebates or over-riders.

Both parties will enter supply partnerships in anticipation of business advantages; the supplier will be keenly seeking additional business that becomes easier to manage and more predictable while the customer will expect cost and operational savings. Rationalisation may be driven by reasons outside the buying remit but should be capable of measuring the benefits.

It is crucial that the process is attended by frequent reviews that define all the associated savings, the direct cost gains that reach the bottom line, and those achieved by improved operational systems (reduced deliveries, less paperwork, lower stock levels). To persuade chief executives that rationalisation has value depends upon realising all, or most, of the original projected cost benefits. These should be identified clearly, by function, by action programme and within an estimated timescale. A constant count on progress is essential, and expected, so that the variances may be understood. It is common for initial expectations to be inaccurate; sometimes failures are balanced by surprise gains. Buying should provide a business case to persuade company support in a normal budgeting manner.

There remains, obstinately, a majority that do not fully check the consequences of supplier rationalisation. It is little wonder that purchasing is fighting a rearguard action when executive ignorance of their activities is perpetuated. In many instances the operational benefits are masked within other company functions (warehousing, stock values) and while this is normal practice it is very important that each saving is identified and associated with the rationalisation programme.

Introducing a new supplier

Markets are fluid and constantly changing; suppliers, market shares, customers and products alter so that supply options will change as well. In a market with static volumes the entry of a new supplier will cause predictable reactions of lowered pricing and the passionate pursuit of customer loyalty. Their arrival may alter the existing business allocations as they provoke gentle expressions of interest from customers who are anxious to gain the advantages of up-to-date production and, probably, predatory pricing.

CHAPTER 3

Selection of suppliers

Given the widespread support for the supply chain management philosophy, the process of supplier selection becomes ever more important. The outdated view, still executed successfully by many supermarket operators, that suppliers would be countenanced only on the basis of price, has been superseded by other factors of commercial relevance.

Gone are the days when buyers would be constrained by the single remit of negotiating prices and general trading terms, leaving the logistics of supply to other functions. The supply chain development has been the most influential feature to impact on purchasing for years. It has made companies aware of the very inefficient process that they suffered and the substantial benefits to be gained from the closer and interwoven relationship with suppliers.

To select a supplier today has ramifications that embrace many different functions and general management is aware that any such selection is a commitment for both parties over a longer period than previously experienced. The independent analysis that accompanies the process has given the purchasing function greater credibility. An integral element in the supply chain arrangement is the measure of supplier performance; the independent measure of each supplier's competence is of critical importance. This has allayed the subjective, but influential, view that the buying department had developed a relationship with their suppliers that could work against the corporate good. Obtaining materials at competitive prices is a purchasing objective but, blindly pursued, may cause costly inefficiencies elsewhere – for example, buying materials and goods that fail to meet the agreed specifications and delivered in a manner that creates additional work for the receiving locations. No company has the capability of handling these costly disruptions. The independent assessment has removed this bias, promoted the proactive relationship with suppliers and been positive in its impact through improving the supply management.

The selection of suppliers with whom the company could develop its future strategies is of great importance and, while remaining the remit of the purchasing department, has become a decision-making process in which many different functions play important roles. The disclosure of corporate plans to an outside operator is an act of trust and can be entered into only with suppliers in whom significant confidence has been established already. The severance of a relationship possesses the same impact – but in reverse. It is incumbent upon those who make such judgements to have a clear understanding of this vital decision. Getting it wrong is going to cause major disruption of every conceivable form – unravelling the electronic linkage, unwinding the technical work and ignoring the knowledge of customers' marketing plans will provide many opportunities for errors. Never before has this facet of the buyer's responsibilities been of such importance. The collaborative attitude of the buying department enables the process to be consensual but with the clear responsibility still resting within the function. The essential precept is to identify those partners capable of staying in total harmony with the customer's corporate objectives for the period of partnership. It is as dramatic and onerous as that! Nothing short of this goal will satisfy the business demands of both participants in the contract. I doubt that there will be many present partnerships able to look back after a decade and vouch that the period has been trouble-free.

The focus of business strategies rarely meets long-term and, frequently, medium-term examination satisfactorily. Therefore the relationship needs to possess an agreed formula for disengagement that removes as many disadvantages as possible.

As potential partners are sought, the most essential element, ethereal though it may be, is the alignment of company philosophies and the necessary financial muscle to fulfil the investment programme required by the customer. The attitudinal similarities form the first hurdle – a simple litmus test of compatibility. These are seeing each other as capable of delivering the parts of each strategic objective through collective action. To illustrate, it would be understandable for packaging companies to seek business links with customers whose market aspirations furthered their own embryonic specialism.

The matching of partners for this purpose should encompass the range of functions but, naturally, purchasing is pre-eminent as the sponsor. The essential communicators on both sides need to have the respect of the other in their professionalism and their ability to translate messages on behalf of the other partner. The channel of communication will become wider and develop between matching functions in each company but the basic business control must remain within the purchasing function. There will need to be clarification, resolution and diplomacy. A critical element will always be the commercial impact on the business relationship and purchasing will be expected to retain absolute responsibility.

The financial well-being of the supplier, and the continuing commitment to investment, especially where technological change is a major and permanent feature, is essential. No worthwhile contract will ever succeed under circumstances that leave either partner uncertain of the other's firm commitment in this area. All too often industry has seen prominent companies pursue a policy to satisfy the 'short-termism' of financial analysts at the expense of maintaining the re-investment necessary to retain and build upon their market position. The supplier needs to have this element as bedrock. The edge available to the customer is heavily based on the low-cost manufacturing capabilities of the supplier and its presence in the vanguard of technical change. If either feature is missing the consequences will slowly become painfully apparent. Financial strength also provides flexibility in the event of the unexpected. Unforeseen variations can be disturbing and the ability to respond effectively is an invaluable asset.

A stimulating and vital ingredient in the trading relationship is the challenge that both parties may bring to the arrangement. With both parties being proactive, in a totally constructive manner, a new and critical dimension beyond the norm is added. It is none the worse for that, as it pushes the players to seek solutions that may not be immediately apparent or which could be difficult. The interaction must demand total concentration from all functions in each company. The modus operandi is to be regularly questioned and challenged. Only under these conditions are real benefits to be achieved. It would be foolish to represent this element as a permanent panacea but the restless pressure generates solutions that provide the commercial edge so essential today.

Although this observation suggests that the customer is the initiator, it is very important for the relationship to be healthy so that the supplier is confident of being an equal partner. This should encourage the challenging of the customer in an atmosphere of confident exchanges. For far too long the natural order has been for this not to be the case and everybody loses. Nothing should be excluded from this examination. Obviously it will become more positive as the relationship develops but it is a necessary opportunity for the supplier to gain confidence from the arrangement.

So important is the consequence for both businesses that in functions that are deemed deficient, especially those of the supplier, it can be helpful for the customer to have a formal right to any new management appointments to be made. It is often found that there are specific weaknesses that need to be resolved for efficient operation. Price competition is normally the easiest measure. However, other elements are very influential and achieving objective judgements as to their effectiveness requires input from other functions. For example, the technical support at the supplier is the internal responsibility of the customer's own equivalent function – purchasing are only able to provide a sketchy judgement. It will be apparent that the consultations will cover a wide range and be very detailed as the courtship develops.

Recognising that most relationships begin to develop with few of the criteria satisfied at the outset it is, however, very important to have the basic prerequisites in position. These would include technical expertise capable of pushing positively towards the customer's business objectives. This function would need to possess commercial understanding, appreciation of the marketing targets and awareness of production constraints and opportunities.

A second element is manufacturing competence so that the products delivered can be immediately processed without any further quality control. As the world moves to self-certification there should be no requirement for such checks. It is pertinent to emphasise the obligation that the supplier accepts under these circumstances, namely that any production that is lost as a consequence of unacceptable materials being delivered could trigger a claim from the customer for lost sales and profit. Focused pressure yields substantial benefits as the producing unit is driven to concentrate.

The customer must have available forecasted requirements to allow the supplier to plan the production utilisation properly. This is a discipline that forces close attention upon the process of estimating future demand. The sales and marketing functions will be expected to provide accurate estimates as the necessary basis for effective supply chain management. All forecasts suffer from variations and these will detract from optimal control.

To complete the major elements in the linking programme is the common ground for the purchasing personnel in both companies, where they meet regularly and debate, discuss and inform each other of the pertinent matters relating to the specific contract. General market conditions including supplies, prices, currencies, competitor activity, etc. will allow purchase judgements to be understood and, if the customer has specific changes in requirements, influenced. There can be no greater benefit than a full knowledge of the circumstances as they affect the purchasing operations. A disparity of abilities is an opportunity to build further benefits into the partnership and not a cause for retreat.

Supplier selection has grown into a process for mutual gain without the disruptive situations that used to thwart such enterprises as pricing quarrels were resolved – always to the chagrin of one protagonist. It would be foolhardy to expect these circumstances to disappear, but the atmosphere should be diffused. Formulated pricing arrangements will never succeed unless the parties have the ability to introduce caveats to reflect the market circumstances. It would be a short-lived relationship if the pricing structure failed to contain this flexibility. The objective for any long-term agreement should ensure that the parties operated on a cost basis equal to, or below, the market levels. Given the savings available through the supply chain initiatives, there would be considerable surprise if the costings were not significantly below the lowest competitor – for material of a similar quality.

Building the relationship will involve combined research and development projects, confidentiality agreement, long-term trading with economic safeguards, knowledge of competitor products and a constant drive for commercial advantage. Suppliers should be capable of bringing added value to the business and each partner must stretch the other's capabilities for mutual commercial benefit. The prime goal is to achieve the competitive edge.

They are hoping to squeeze you so close they'll squeeze all your profit away. How do you know when you're at the optimum cost? Who says how much profit you can make? At the end of the day, it's the big company; you have no power. (Supplier)

The ultimate objective of supply partnerships is achieving, collectively, a market position that beats or matches the most competitive alternative. It is naive to imagine that this laudable goal cannot be reached in a painless manner; both parties will contribute skills as well as blood, sweat and tears. The target will be reached only by close collaboration, so that each party benefits.

The obvious alternative is to pressurise the supply chain to, and beyond, breaking point without any operational support except ill-disguised buying power. This is viable in markets where the products are easily produced and characterised by too many suppliers. Hitting sitting targets is not difficult but the challenge and satisfaction of supply relationships is to achieve lower costs in a financially secure partnership that moves each company forward beyond competition and retains an attraction to other potential suppliers.

Sometimes, however, there are insufficient suppliers to allow the selection process to take place. For various reasons there may be no immediate business partners available and the choices include assisting a supplier, from those presently active, to improve their situation for your business benefit or to encourage a current non-participant to invest and become a newly established supplier of the required material. In the first instance, it may be conceivable for internal advisors to support the development of the chosen supplier and, subject to the financial cost of establishing a greenfield site operation, your company may enter into a joint venture arrangement.

CHAPTER 4

Managing the external suppliers

Introduction

Suppliers are an essential prerequisite to the health of any business. As providers of goods and services that form the base on which company activities are built, they represent the largest element of cost and, potentially, are the most valuable asset. As value is added to purchased goods and services, the prosperity of any business depends upon the relationships with suppliers and customers. Their importance is pivotal and mistakes can be terminal. Failing to deliver on time and delivering out-of-specification materials are simple illustrations of potential calamities. The present drive towards low stock levels held cumulatively throughout the supply chain will magnify every problem and could result in serious trouble.

Success, however, is created by establishing positive links with both groups; the customers to appreciate and demand products and the suppliers to align their business for mutual commercial benefit.

Suppliers are the extension to a company and, therefore, should be handled as an integral ally in meeting business objectives. They have the critical responsibility of providing goods and services that meet the agreed specification every time. Therefore, selecting the most appropriate suppliers demands considerable care, even though seeking out those who are kindred spirits and espouse similar objectives is time-consuming and onerous. Building empathy with the major suppliers is very important because it frequently yields substantial advantages that do not appear on any invoices. It is unwieldy and unnecessary to extend collaboration to every supplier because of the differing values they contribute. Those elements of service that are deemed special will highlight the suppliers to whom extra attention should be given.

The role of purchasing

Purchasing is the 'lead' function in selecting and establishing effective relationships with external suppliers. The determination of preferred sourcing is a shared activity but the purchasing function retains the responsibility of managing, nurturing and promoting the relationship in an effort to provide commercial advantages to the company. Internal debates have caused great resentment whenever purchasing has pursued a unilateral course; imagine the logistical problems suffered by production in the pursuit of lowest cost supplies. Supplier evaluation practices had their fountain-spring from concerns about production efficiency that was impacted by imperfect servicing from suppliers. There is no doubt that such measures have created confidence among internal functions.

The early essays into just-in-time have delivered amazing logistical benefits that directly swelled profits by reducing stocks held throughout the supply chain. Each component activity added positive benefits and encouraged the development of partnerships. However, unbridled enthusiasm for short-term joint ventures could tempt many companies into unsuitable relationships that greater care and planning would have avoided. It is very important to 'make haste slowly'. Interlinking stock control systems is the first step towards closer functional activities and should be viewed as a serious commitment for the future. Modern philosophy underpinning lean supply strategies places great importance on the seamless supply of parts that combine to produce the final marketed product. This is available only in a totally integrated scheme.

Every company performs a variety of activities that require a disparate range of services provided by their suppliers. In consequence, the character of the supplier base differs as the complexity of these requirements varies.

In simplistic markets driven by 'generic' performance needs there is, understandably, a concentration on price-competition and little concern about the technical requirements. In circumstances that demand the eschewing of expensive peripheral activities and total concentration on cost efficiencies there is an overwhelming need for shared pursuit of performance improvements. To aspire towards lowest cost inevitably requires total collaboration between the interdependent manufacturers that represent the supply chain.

Purchasing performs the filtration process that determines the width and quality of the inter-company information exchange. The extent and nature of this relationship will depend upon a developed confidence and shared targets reached through mutual interaction and support. The fullest relationship would be described as a partnership in which the companies become interdependent. Handled badly, the relationship will generate pain, inefficiencies and, ultimately, separation! The supplier should be encouraged to not only bring new ideas and products to their customer but also positive contributions to the essential drive for efficiencies in operations and purchasing. The supplier should be encouraged to challenge dictates from the customer whenever these are felt to be counter-productive. Those functions demonstrably inter-dependent in the relationship are purchasing/logistics and new product development/quality control.

Every marriage is threatened by divorce, especially in this modern social environment, and the partners should have an agreed procedure to follow if this possibility becomes a reality. The protection of discreet knowledge between the parties is extremely difficult but must be considered inviolate. This illustrates the importance of purchasing's role in managing and encouraging the relationship to grow for the benefit of both parties.

This book is designed to examine the most extensive relationship so that, depending upon your judgement of the special circumstances pertinent to your own supplier base, these may be adopted partially or wholly.

Qualities of suppliers

These companies are the 'uncosted' assets of your company's strength; they provide a range of support that, if properly managed, will deliver substantial benefits to the operations. The better suppliers will perform substantial additional tasks in support of the business level and prospects that you represent.

They are the outsourced element of your purchasing function and ignoring the substantial impact that their buying decisions have on the cost of imported goods and services is disastrous. The variation in purchased costs is directly influencing the bottom line and, therefore, their purchasing abilities are key to the efficiency of your business. It takes little time to recognise that, fallible as we all are, the suppliers' poor buying decisions result in added expenses to their customers! *Beware the supplier whose poor buying capabilities saddle your company with unrecoverable input costs.* Knowledge of the buying personnel, their capabilities and the markets that they use for their sourcing is crucial.

In addition, the supplying company must have purchasing strategies that are 'in line' with your own; the most obvious discrepancy is in unrestricted decision-making for the buyers with reference to general management. It is often a reflection of the business trading module or, very simplistically, one calendar year.

The easiest and most powerful illustration is mineral oil. Every student of this market would recognise that at $10 per barrel the odds were heavily stacked in favour of increasing price levels so that, cautious or otherwise, the buyer would have been keen to obtain extended hedge protection. When prices surge beyond $30 per barrel everybody becomes a sudden expert. *You need to be and, inevitably, so does your supplier!* Shared judgements demonstrate a cohesion between companies and not the reverse; accept that many of your 'better' buying assessments will be imparted to your potential competitors through this shared activity but it should never prevent you from exercising these options for your own company's benefit. The practice of joining the purchasing decisions will, in the fullness of time, convince the buying staff of your support and understanding of their function. Solid relationships will follow and confidence will be built.

The highest expression of a working partnership that will endure is the arrangement under which, given clear undisputed evidence of comparable and competitive offerings, your supplier is committed to matching the 'best' market quotation. Never knowingly undersold is an objective for all commercial enterprises and, given the openness of today's marketplace, the publicity that attends major price movements and sharp competition will easily provide this knowledge. Meeting competition has many facets and should be analysed to your satisfaction.

Funding modern businesses continues to rise; new techniques, capital equipment, computerisation, legal constraints all force the cost of building viable enterprises upwards. Frequently, the less wealthy companies protect their market position by driving prices down and living off lower margins. In such circumstances, the available finance for any new initiative is not available and a lingering death follows. Suppliers incapable of keeping pace with the changes may have an invaluable place in the purchasing scheme but it will never be based on long-term expectations! The coat must be cut according to the cloth so that each supplier performs a different role.

CHAPTER 5

Discharging buying responsibilities

Introduction

Many purchasing units possess strategies that have been accepted by the company and the following statements reflect the general principles adopted.

- *To purchase goods and services at the lowest cost commensurate with the specification and service levels.*

    Sharpen the focus and show the world what you can do! Your internal customers will have a simple direct and uncompromising attitude to the functional achievements. Pay prices above those of your competitors and seek another job as soon as possible. Beyond the plethora of additional factors within the buying remit is the unchanging objective of contributing lowest prices!

    It should promote a debate as to the purchasing remit. It is an outdated philosophy that allows other company functions to continue exercising a purchasing activity without any input from the function itself. To buy goods and services, and especially service, in isolation ignores the lack of specialist purchasing techniques and permits the supplier to benefit, sometimes enormously, from this blinkered approach. The collaboration between the requisitioning function and purchasing could yield measurable gains. It is puerile to pretend otherwise.

- *To reduce supply chain costs to the minimum operational level.*

  Examining each segment of activity will quickly identify duplication, repetition and irrelevant, outdated procedures that do not contribute to business effectiveness. The review will indicate alternative activities (stocks, paperwork, communication) to minimise costs. This objective is totally interdependent and relies on internal support as well as supplier assistance.

- *To source goods and services from suppliers who will enhance the added-value elements through technical development and supply servicing.*

  Regular review forums, including technical staff from the supplier, are essential for efficient management of this situation. Ill-defined and undisciplined projects cause damage; small project groups formed and reformed at regular intervals should keep the business 'on its toes' and alert to alternative options. Imaginative and questioning teams provide the motivation for progress. Business vitality is maintained as the objectives alter; being stuck in a rut dulls the senses and diminishes focus.

  Speaking to the world via the Internet carries information overload; there is much dross but also gold dust. Purchasing staff interact with suppliers and markets abroad and at home so that news is constantly delivered.

  The simplest illustration relates directly to the goods or services bought by an individual buyer and the future expectations of availability, price, new suppliers or alternative products.

Obviously it is facile to assume, for planning purposes, that the world is unchanging; marketing managers cannot extrapolate the present into the future with constant prices for all supplies and be annoyed and irritated when the reality proves very different! Information flow is important for internal functions as much as that received by external suppliers. Advance information is important; the erection of tariff barriers would batter the company planning and preventative action is required. No buyer should be caught unawares.

Buying never ceases and there is no time at which the search for improved costs or service ends. Every buyer believing on the day after a deal has been struck that there could have been improvements reflects this situation. Hence the constant pressing for further benefits. The signed contract is never the conclusion.

Buyers are restless souls attempting to remain in the vanguard to yield benefits for their company equal to the best. A special art form is to obtain credit as if your company was ten times larger. Taking advantage of others' ignorance is a signal warning against your own lack of up-to-date information!

Ever-present negotiations

If these comments strike a chord, then you will realise that knowledge is power, and a clear understanding of the cost profile for purchased goods and services is crucial to obtaining tactical advantages in the negotiations. It is very important to understand the supplier's cost profile, the general market levels and the further improvements that can be obtained; it is difficult to imagine that the buyer will possess all this information, but, buying 'blind' is ignorant. The frequency at which discussions or negotiations occur will be dictated by the changing marketplaces for the finished products or bought-in materials. When buying aluminium foil, for instance, one would expect an understanding of the metal market prices, currency movements and the contracted cover of the supplier. It is conceivable that joint decisions concerning contracting for base metal supplies would occur so that the customer, sharing in this process, would obtain pricing to reflect the shared choice, for good or ill. Buying at the bottom of a market is a gift of the gods and not normal practice for buyers; buying within sight of a market low point should be achievable.

Many practitioners have described the initial discussions for a new product or service as exploring the 'ground' and assessing the parameters for the discussions. Each party will be trying to assess the sharpness of the negotiators and deciding the limits beyond which pressure becomes counter-productive. Finding the 'back wall' is a key exercise that may remain 'live' for several meetings; the 'wall' is the point at which the supplier will 'fold up his bed and walk away'. Skilled buying stops short of this climactic situation through a combination of knowledge (market, materials, competition, cost profiling and the supplier's profitability) and understanding the business attractions being presented to the potential supplier.

The 'game' is always live

Market circumstances are never static and professional buying should have a monitoring function to maintain the level of competition for the customer and the supplier. Collaboration is advantageous and the supplier may welcome information concerning competitive levels to improve their internal performances further.

Find those with executive power

It is absolutely vital that negotiations take place with the supplier representative possessing executive power. Aimless discussions with salespeople who refer all decisions to their absent manager is disastrous – negotiations may be half-finished, negotiating positions exposed and all elements of unusual tactics 'blown'. Meeting powerless representatives under these circumstances is a useless and indictable offence!

Patience with a company representative who is charming but lacks any ability to make decisions confidently and speedily should wear thin very quickly. While personal relationships are important in building a favourable business ambience, time pressures are so great that meetings yielding no progress should be avoided like the plague. It is also the case that every meeting is not a matter of life or death *but* all discussions with other companies should have managers capable of exercising power to move the business forward. Conversely it is incumbent upon your company to respond directly; early tentative approaches will anticipate a protracted 'courtship' but reflect a lack of executive power. Yet modern businesses continue to sanction inefficient purchasing procedures that damage their image. Administrative staff performing the buying role without possessing power causes serious frustration for suppliers.

Negotiating strategies

Pre-arranged objectives must be in place and agreed before any debates take place. To enter any discussion in an unprepared state deserves dismissal and poorly constructed agreements that favour the supplier. Never buy in a vacuum, because the decision will not allow assessment as to the effectiveness of the judgement. Many buyers adopt tactics of reducing any quotation from the supplier regardless of reality. A discount is only a *relative* expression and the buyer should establish from what level it is being measured.

It is intelligent to adjust the negotiating stance depending upon the power balance. To strut and posture with little prospect of success is extremely damaging. Battles are to be won on surer ground! Well-briefed buying will impress the supplier and achieve good results. Ignorance, therefore, is a licence to take advantage.

There will be instances when the buyer needs to use a supplicant mode. All the tactical strength is with their supplier and little advantage is available. Tactics should be to divert the discussion into other supply factors from which the customer would like to gain, while conceding the pricing situation.

Psychological warfare

Managing people is a skill-set that requires some understanding of human behaviour patterns and attitudes. It sometimes seems bizarre to believe that salespeople can be influenced by small social ploys but, in general, the non-confrontational approach gives some, albeit small, advantage for the buyer. Conceding a price, on the assumption that the salesperson is committed to achieving this particular target, can yield considerable benefits in the provision of extra services that carry little or no cost. It is a game and playing it with skill and sensitivity can deliver accolades from the supplier as to the warm, shared visions that buyers and salespeople enjoy.

Keeping the initiative is crucial

Punching above your weight is the objective of all buyers. Gaining an exaggerated advantage is the target; act like a multinational and the fruits will arrive.

A wide range of influences that change continuously affects the cost of imported goods and services. Currency exchange rates, national and international legislation and politics combine to impact upon the invoiced costs of goods and services. Each element deserves attention because any consequent cost increase needs to be both recovered from customers and attended by a valid account provided by the purchasing function, and any reduction should be enjoyed from the moment of implementation!

The buying role is pivotal and relies upon the support of other company functions for the fullest effectiveness; for example, technicians define and defend the minimum company quality standards, production managers determine the efficacy of alternative products and marketing staff exchange information on alternative materials being developed or being used by competition. Persuading internal customers is the key practice of proactive buyers.

Creating choice that can be exercised by other company departments is an important gambit. The power of making decisions is enjoyable and, while the commercial differences have been removed through negotiations, the option to select a supplier builds a favourable atmosphere. Secretaries and personal assistants are powerful and have preferences for the supply, for example, of stationery so that supply agreements that have two alternative suppliers are desirable. To restrict choice to a single supplier is politically dangerous and may be wittingly derailed. Tempting assassination is foolish!

Empowering the internal customers wins friends and supporters at no cost and improves the departmental performance enormously! For low-value repetitive orders it is efficient to negotiate 'blanket' contracts at agreed prices from which company individuals may order directly. The order will be initiated internally, transmitted electronically, delivered, invoiced and paid automatically without involving purchasing. The perception appeals to all and each element is efficient.

The theory in favour of supplier rationalisation is extremely attractive. Reducing supplier numbers should automatically endow the remaining suppliers with increased business. The rationalisation will be attended by a price reduction that stretches into an assured future. There are innumerable positive logistics benefits, such as fewer deliveries, lower administration, etc., but the increased volume should result in lower prices.

Different industries and markets may argue for variations on this theme. Single suppliers with several manufacturing units capable of supply should be seen as a multiple sourcing arrangement. Certainty of supply should rank highly and these options will be keenly demanded. Rationalisation is endemic and all companies within the supply chain will be performing the same process. In consequence the lines of supply may be severely constrained against any previous situation. Approval of supplying points by the internal quality control (QC) function will monitor the changes but the emergency alternatives should be clearly understood.

The only established measuring system compares your forecasted savings against the present situation. These benefits may be provided in different guises and are dependent upon the importance of each supplier. Those who are unimportant may be encouraged to offer terms in advance of the trading period, regular backdated rebates or overriders, etc.

Rationalisation may be driven by reasons outside the buying remit but the scheme should expect measurable gains.

Price is the key issue

Any buyer entering negotiations with a weaker knowledge base than the supplier is doomed. Information is the permanent requirement for effective buying. Buying techniques are a separate subject but the managing of suppliers will involve several tactics. Anticipating market movements and your suppliers' intentions will reward careful study; indeed, markets affecting every element of the goods and services are important. Buyers should be very widely read and possess an exhaustive contact list. Advice from every market participant is valuable; care is essential because there will be observers whose purpose is to regurgitate, parrot-fashion, general market commentaries without the slightest analysis, understanding or appreciation for your position! Reject these charlatans as soon as possible. The job is to select those people who can contribute positively to your task of out-thinking your competition. Read everything and select, subsequently, the publications that serve your purpose best. In today's world of information overload there is plenty that can be consigned to the rubbish bin immediately.

It is important to recognise that business pressures impact upon all participants equally. In consequence, there is no justification for any special pleading by any special interest company or supplier. Their reward is in the business they enjoy from your patronage. The tough market that they, and you, have joined voluntarily allows no free rides and the pressures have to be transferred into the search for advantages. As the salesperson is a mirror reflection of the buyer it will be important to understand his or her objectives for each meeting. He or she will represent their employer and it is good tactics to anticipate their approach.

In every contract renewal situation there is a historical performance that is available to assess the service and quality capabilities. There will be new potential suppliers whose products and qualities have been measured. The awarding process includes all elements but special attention is given to pricing and the guarantees that the supplier will accept throughout the contract period so that you will enjoy a continuous advantage. Whether a Dutch auction or ITT (invitation to tender) directs the adjudication process, the final award is price-driven.

CHAPTER 6

Outsourced purchasing

The modern vogue

Current economic theory is dominated by the lean slim company philosophy that retains in-house control on the mainstream activities, directly contributing to their perceived USP (unique selling proposition), while subcontracting to outside management the responsibility for indirect costs. This is based upon the belief that managers should focus on their specialist skills and contract out the peripheral activities to external agencies. Activities that most easily suit the outsourcing process would include IT operations, estate management, call centres, human resources and logistics.

The economic benefits will include (a) a reduction in company headcount as most outsourcing projects are accompanied by the transfer of staff; (b) shortening corporate reaction times as specialist contractors perform their functions more effectively; and (c) freeing management to concentrate on the real business without any decline in service levels. Managed with clearly defined responsibilities for the subcontractor and effective control by the principal, this process yields positive benefits.

A leading London hospital, Great Ormond Street, outsourced its stationery supplies to save 'time, money and warehouse space'. Previously the hospital had bought stationery in bulk and stored against demand. While the cost of low-value items represented 3–5% of purchasing expenditure, the processing of orders in-house needed two full-time staff. One was retained to focus on strategic purchasing and the other moved to another department. 'From processing 100 invoices each week we deal with one'.

Princes Soft Drinks has contracted with water company experts to (a) minimise the amount of water being used within their production processes and the ensuing effluent; and (b) reduce existing tariffs for the fresh supplies.

The gospel of outsourcing has been enthusiastically embraced. Executive imaginations are captured by the vision and it has successfully persuaded companies to outsource many supporting activities beyond their core business. Economic commentators have extrapolated the fashion trend into virtual companies holding little beyond a corporate dream! Indeed, when British Airways began unbundling their corporate structure in 1998 it was suggested that the company name alone could be totally supported through the outsourcing of every activity, including the aircraft and staff.

During the preparations for outsourcing a review of those functions to be transferred provides the opportunity to discuss, debate and affirm their essential activities and value to the company. It is an elegant illustration of the benefits to be derived from internal consultancy so that, prior to the transfer of responsibility being performed, a clear updated definition for each function is obtained. This should form the basis for the contractual terms.

Inevitably this is an oversimplification, but it provides some understanding for the potentially disastrous consequences of outsourcing functions without sufficient thought and analysis. In the rush to transfer executive power, the subcontractor may be given too much freedom and a poorly specified operating brief. According to research, 41% of outsourcing contracts fail to make any transition or transfer provision for either the customer or supplier to exit the contract when it is due for termination!

A serious deficiency is the lack of consideration given to possible changes in business circumstances. The commercial world is fluid and companies may alter shape and ownership with a rapidity that often defies conventional logic. The contractual agreement, therefore, needs to anticipate the unexpected and contain preventative clauses that reinforce the principal's control.

In late 2000, Cornhill, a British insurance company, announced the intention to bring IT purchasing back in-house in a bid to 'improve service levels and cut costs'. The outsourcing, three years previously, was performed to cut overheads and 'there was a perception that it was a quick, easy and cheaper solution which would allow the company to focus on its core business. But things have changed'!

Following a major rail disaster in which four people died, Railtrack, responsible for the track and signalling systems of British railways, is reviewing the outsourcing of railway maintenance. 'We thought we had a process that meant contractors would bring up problems such as cracked rails. Clearly we can't rely on that process anymore so we are undertaking a comprehensive review of our contracting arrangements,' they said.

> Railtrack, the embattled infrastructure group, will come under further pressure today when operating companies qualify for a new way of claiming compensation from it. Yesterday marked six months to the day since the fatal Hatfield accident. Under a little-noticed clause in the operator's contract, any 'temporary' deterioration in the condition of the network lasting more than six months is deemed to have become permanent, and operators can claim for long-term lost business. Railtrack says the rule applies only to specific speed restrictions and future losses. But lawyers for at least one big operator believe the state of the network would qualify and claims could be retrospective. Virgin Trains, which operates the West Coast London–Scotland main line, could start proceedings this week. Virgin claims Railtrack will owe it

£100m for lost business in the first year after last October's accident. Railtrack rejects the claim. Yesterday Virgin insiders said hopes of avoiding legal arbitration or court proceedings were fading. National Express and GNER have, also, threatened legal action. (*Financial Times*, April 2001)

Without a careful and cautious approach it becomes a recipe for impending disaster – from which only lawyers benefit!

However, for those who shrug with disdain as they view the discomfiture of their headstrong competitors, spare a thought for the outsourcing activity that everyone has been constantly supporting, namely the purchasing activities performed by their suppliers!

The unchanging version

pass the parcel
when the music stops you're out...
...disadvantaged and dead!

Creating a competitive edge is a constant concern for every business and few markets, if any, can provide relief. The steady attack on all forms of market collaboration has removed many old protective fences that gave surety of profits. To reach this objective requires, as an essential prerequisite, an admirably sharp operational cost base, and, while every corporate activity will contribute, the cost impact of purchased items is massive and constant.

In manufacturing companies the standard cost profile details purchases (goods, materials and services) as representing 70% of the final cost. There are no other elements that compare with this level of importance so that the purchasing function is thrust into the limelight. In companies where buying is fragmented and performed by several different functions, e.g. marketing organising media advertising and engineers purchasing capital equipment, this factor may be masked and misunderstood. Most importantly, however, the impact is truly crucial.

Purchasing has to recognise that every invoice – received, approved and paid – contains the aggregate of each buying decision made to that point in the supply chain. The buyers have, by proxy, discharged those decisions, for good or ill, in an outsourced manner! The enormity of this situation demands urgent attention. And herein lies the problem!

Buying is an imperfect art; misjudgements exist and there will be additional costs to be borne. The misjudgements will involve many different factors such as variable requirements (too much, too little, too early, too late), incorrect specifications, currency changes, misreading market movements etc. These mistakes, however, need to be recovered if the profit target is to be reached; hence, to buy well allows the company to sell well!

Each company in the supply chain will buy materials and services with their buying staff sharing the common aforementioned circumstances. The implication is that the full supply chain possesses a 'thread' of additional costs, imperfections multiplied, which exist naturally and are transferred from one link in the chain to the next, such that the ultimate link carries the accumulated costs. In an extreme situation the buying staff, at the supplier, may have misjudged market price movements and, consequently, be paying a higher price for materials that will form a part, small or large, of product that will subsequently be sold to the customer. This error of judgement will be included in the invoiced price and passed forward down the supply chain. *There may be several different tactics to 'squeeze this cost sausage' but no obvious opportunity of excluding it completely!*

Buyers should be totally indignant that they absorb such errors but the reality dictates otherwise! Recently British Gas was severely embarrassed by an unexpected decline in crude oil pricing that exposed their existing supply contracts. The disparity between contracted and market price levels was so large that the commercial distortion raised serious business problems. The Industry Regulator, appointed by the government to oversee the privatisation of this energy market, became involved and suggested that British Gas customers should 'shoulder' the cost differential burden, thereby giving an official sanction for a contractual mistake. *This illustrates the ongoing inevitability of transferring supplier misjudgements. These errors (a) will be undefined, (b) may be large and (c) could/should be discharged against less demanding customers.*

Knowledge is power and the buying operation at the supplier must be fully understood. Any buyer who does not comprehend the circumstances of his or her functional colleagues is dangerously negligent. There will be operational differences that, of their own existence, implicitly introduce problems. These differences include personal buying skills, corporate constraints on buying authority in both time and value, and the administration of currency requirements. The range and complexity of these approaches can be awesome and daunting; they are, however, extremely important and possess potentially significant cost consequences.

Each buyer should, therefore, have the opportunity to understand, and the option of participating in, those decisions exercised by their immediate supplier. To do otherwise is to accept the judgement of their buying colleagues and that is foolhardy. Buyers must fully appreciate the parameters within which their colleagues operate.

Company operating manuals will specify limits for purchasing commitments directed by financial managers. These controls will normally be expressed through the volume of the commitments and the period they represent against the ongoing company forecasts. The latter is usually expressed as the annual usage. The company trading module, normally a year, is critical for senior management and captures the greatest attention when major purchasing decisions are demanded.

Working within these corporate guidelines buyers will strive to secure the best commercial deals that will reflect their judgement in assessing, predicting, managing and accepting costs.

Those buying decisions, shared with suppliers, are easiest to describe through futures markets, which are mirror images of normal physical trade and have developed in response to the widespread need for traders (producers, agents, consumers and speculators) to obtain some pricing certainty beyond the short-term period in which the physical business is transacted. In London there are futures markets in soft commodities (coffee, cocoa), metals (platinum), currencies and mineral oils. The ultimate user will frequently choose to trade in the futures markets through their physical suppliers and the trading decisions will be collectively studied and debated before implementation. It demonstrates collaboration and separates these shared decisions from the physical business between the companies. The alternative option is to trade directly into the futures market, which transfers all financial obligations to the customer; this may cause finance serious concerns of exposure, margin call and allocation of market losses. Many companies are risk-averse and, given the dramatic and colourful stories of massive failures in the futures markets, will require considerable persuasion before participation is considered.

Long-term students and analysts of mineral oil market prices will provide excellent guidance on the probabilities associated with contracting mineral oil forward at the $10/barrel or $30/barrel levels. Due to the multiple applications for oil (energy, plastic packaging, etc.) the opportunity to obtain protection against major negative cost movements is welcome. Plastics producers purchase polystyrene granules or oil derivatives that reflect these price movements and, with an agreed commitment from their customers, have the ability to ensure extended supplies that yield substantial market price advantages. Should a few industrial giants in non-confrontational mode provide these supplies, this tactic becomes more valuable. It is obvious that 'long' contracted supplies will be enormously beneficial if priced on $10/barrel raw material costs! Buyers recognising the potential of such market opportunities will drive their company into an extremely competitive situation. Inevitably this will generate business advantages to the supplier, who will obtain greater volume requirements.

Similarly, if, for example, protection is needed against currency movements, the customer may request that the supplier manages a hedge programme on their behalf. Normal practice is to accept any negative consequences, or losses, to be included in (added to) the invoices and profits directly transferred. Exchange rates remain unpredictable but impact heavily on international trading companies, whether they purchase or sell abroad. Every company should manage the currency exposure not by any emotional expectation or beliefs of their financial senior managers but through a mechanistic programme that removes human judgements from the process.

Buyers in both companies will seek the lowest cost commensurate with the corporate standards or specifications for quality and service. The buyer will negotiate on an amalgam of factors that contribute to the final invoiced price, payment terms, and delivery formats, etc., and be wholly responsible. Common practice is for the invoiced price to be measured against the internal company budget that has been established for the relevant trading period, normally the financial year. However, as everyone recognises, this is less than absolute because (a) the buyer will have contributed to the construction of the budget, and/or (b) there is no reliable objective system to measure reality against competitor activity or the market.

To understand and share the environment, challenges and opportunities with the supplier's buyers offer the chance of substantial cost improvements.

The driving force should be to reach the most competitive possible arrangement every time. The collaborative activity will have different forms; the most awkward example is when the ultimate customer directs their supplier(s) to selected sources with whom they have an arrangement providing 'hidden' discounts for the consequent business derived from the intermediary company. It does, however, enable a 'small' supplier to obtain materials or products at price levels that, alone, would have been unattainable, even allowing for the 'hidden' discounts.

In most instances the supplier operates to a different contract commitment timescale from their customer and, in consequence, is reluctant to accept extended obligations on the uncertain basis that their customer will support this atypical arrangement, especially when the costs associated with this special arrangement move against the original intention. The relationship is challenged under these circumstances! Confidence in a partner's attitude in loss situations must exist before this situation merits contemplation. Disowning informal agreements leads the innocents to an early death!

Knowledge of the supplier's purchasing function is essential. This is a collaborative stance and should not be viewed as intrusive. It should be seen as supportive and promoted as seeking mutual advantage. It is obvious that customer satisfaction is needed and open discussion concerning the purchasing procedures, judgements and constraints will assist rather than detract from that objective. The sole rationale is to avoid every cost penalty, particularly if that derives from poor performances by the supplier's buying staff!

Challenging the professional expertise of functional 'fellow-travellers' is difficult but here, however, it is critical. Shared analysis of a common market allows the opportunity of improving buying decisions. The same materials or products may have different values that are managed by different buying skills; implicit is the chance that combined assessment will outweigh singular attention. To share 'supply partnerships' or the old-fashioned confrontational buying process without this necessary examination leaves buyers adrift from reality. It is the ignored feature in demonstrating buying excellence missed by friend and foe alike!

To contemplate this sensitive action epitomises a close supplier–customer relationship.

It is most unlikely to succeed with customers who lack any forecasting accuracy or who may have several potential suppliers for whom gaining favour depends on their cost competitiveness. Unless the supplier has confidence in both the relationship and their customer's forecasting, this debate will be fraught and potentially dangerous. Nobody enjoys possessing contracted commitments at prices above the subsequent market levels and evasive shuffling of feet will do nothing to restore the fragile inter-company confidence. It is not recommended for the early stages of confidence building but fits the advanced circumstances under which 'losses', and their absorption, are clearly identified and accepted. Inevitably examples of mini-disasters abound and should the customer be capable of renegotiating previously agreed contracts without recognising their obligations, the consequences are self-evident.

We live in a world besotted with technical innovation and hype, where businesses are being lured by enthusiastic proponents of electronic software, while lying untouched and unnoticed is the greatest prize available to the buyers, namely an insight into a world they, themselves, understand very well! This is the buying challenge discharged, on their behalf, by those empowered to exercise the same judgement for the suppliers. Strange that such obvious shared problems and opportunities have lain unexamined to the disadvantage of all within the supply chain!

No constructive work has been performed in evaluating this serious risk area. How slow the buying function is to manage this hazard!

CHAPTER 7

Contracts

Introduction

The contract is a written statement that describes the material or service being provided by the supplier to the customer. The obligations of the customer could be included. It may be reviewed regularly or spasmodically and, with consent, be altered. It is an important document in the event of a disagreement.

Appearing in law courts is expensive, protracted and disastrous for public relations. Every sinew should be strained to reach a settlement; agreement is almost always preferable to dispute. Each contract will vary but, throughout, there are common clauses to be included. They should define responsibilities and the consequences for any failure.

Standard terms and conditions

Specifications

- *Agreed details of product/service to be provided.* The specifications will include performance guarantees. This section is open to uncertainty and, subject to arguments, will require an independent assessor to provide arbitrary judgement. If, for example, using materials results in processing problems, and a consequential loss in, say, factory efficiencies, this can be determined as lost profit. The supplier will need insurance cover for any shortfall, whether there is a claim or not.

- At present there are quality checks on receipt that form the first acceptance level. This is not total acceptance because products that achieve the physical specification do not always satisfy subsequent operational procedures. Where these processes are important, there should be additional clauses that extend the specification.

- In circumstances where products are supplied to form a part component for a complex assembly there is, in my opinion, considerable justification for being supplied with multiple components from a single supply source to reduce the arguments that follow any failure; using products from separate sources leads to inconclusive debates and an inability to recover lost revenues. Buyers will be exercised to achieve the lowest complete pricing if this stance is adopted. Other functions should be expected to decide on the tactics.

- It is an essential prerequisite of supply chain management that the supplier should deliver product within specification and, thereby, remove the need for any quality inspection. It eliminates the requirement for QC, cuts inventory to minimum levels and penalises the supplier for any production inefficiencies.

- The document should be dated and signed by both companies. It is important that all changes be maintained in an up-to-date fashion.

Period of contract

- There is general acceptance that contract terms of less than three years do not allow supply chain benefits to be identified and captured. The process of establishing the electronic data interchange (EDI) links and ensuring the open flow of information to the supplier can be a slow educational process. Functions within the client organisation discover the responsibilities they now have for ensuring that forecasted requirements are as accurate as possible.

- It is becoming apparent that partners who have developed a close working relationship can contemplate five years as the contract period. It is inevitable that business planning will become less clear as the timescale extends. The variation will be greater, for example, in forecasted volumes. Industry is always fluid and plants can be sold or closed as well as companies acquired so that the contract should allow annual revisions of future expectations.

- Every contract will allow a termination clause that gives each signatory the option of abandoning the arrangement – under certain specified circumstances. These may vary considerably but will always include failure to agree on pricing. For the normal contract of three years the termination would be three months. As the relationship becomes closer administratively, the more difficult it is to contemplate 'divorce'. Supply chain links deliver a strong commitment from the customer and should provide the supplier with a sense of confidence.

Volume projections

- Each contract will include a forecast of volumes expected through its lifetime. To predict for either three or five years is perceived as difficult, if not impossible, but a contract should not exclude volume forecasts. Promotional activity, unpredictable behaviour by the retail customers and the industrial changes in manufacturing sites will be elements of general uncertainty. The supplier will be challenged and the response will need to be very positive if the contract provokes investment decisions.

- While the contract is running the customer will seek to operate to the shortest period of commitment to firm volumes. Under the normal supply chain agreements there are several forecasts – the longer the period involved, the greater the variability. The standard working period is 13 weeks, within which there is a firm committed period of six to eight weeks during which the customer will accept the forecasted volumes. The remainder of the period will be subject to a ±10% variation.

- If the customer is seeking a rebate deal it is probable that the annual contractual volumes will be low so as to create an attractive rebate arrangement. If agreed, the deal would use the first year's volume to form the basis for the following year's rebate calculations, and so on. The rebate has tremendous attractions for the customer as it is (a) withheld from the sales personnel who might, otherwise, concede it to their clients, and (b) provides the finance department with flexibility in allocating corporate profits. The danger for suppliers in this process is that, once agreed, the customer could request the rebate to be deducted from the delivery invoices – on the basis that the supplier is clearly capable of conceding further ground on pricing!

Pricing mechanism

- Contract pricing is based upon publicly available independent market databases. The contract will include mechanisms that trigger pricing discussions. It would be unusual for the contract to have an automatic price adjustment that precluded any debate.

- A wide range of agreements is possible but most will include the buyer's right to challenge the existing pricing if the market quotations are available at a discount to the contract level, perhaps in excess of 5%. The tactic for the buyer is to ensure that the supplier remains competitive. Under sole supply agreements, this will be written in stone!

- If the market were to rise, the seller will seek a price increase and the discussions will follow familiar lines. The buyer will seek to (a) minimise the increase; (b) delay its implementation; and (c) use every element of market information to dismiss the request.

- It would be for the supplier to create a contractual statement of costs for the manufacture of the product that is accepted by the customer so that the margin can be directly sustained. Any contract based on a 'cost-plus' principle will give the supplier considerable benefits from the negotiations.

Penalty clauses

- All penalty clauses will operate against the supplier and be based upon customer service. This principle is well advanced industrially and acceptable to the contract parties. The most effective measurements are (a) deliveries on time with (b) goods of acceptable quality. In efficient companies there is a desire to provide valuable performance data without adding significant administration costs. This is not a universally accepted principle as managers are tempted to extend the measurements and produce complex computer-based programs.

- Simple measures are capable of assisting suppliers in their logistics management and provide customers with invaluable information that affords independent assessment of suppliers – and acts as a useful negotiating tool. Many companies are working with these measurement systems and will understand the inclusion in a contract.

- Penalty clauses are not universally used. Customers should expect that the suppliers achieving better results in the customer service scheme would gain more business from their weaker brethren. However, there are some penalty arrangements where supplies fail to achieve an accepted target. They take the form of alternative supply deals (e.g. additional product at reduced costs). There are many options. It will be expected that suppliers attain ever improving standards until – finally – they have reached a level beyond which there is no commercial benefit to be obtained.

- 'Total quality' has been removed from corporate objectives in Japan now that it has been reached.

- The installation of capital equipment requires specific performance guarantees that will define the technical and operational capabilities of the purchased equipment. It will require agreed measures for the installation in terms of time, costs and the provision of facilities by the buying company. Each party will need to assess the commercial consequences of late delivery and installation, substandard performances by the equipment and the liabilities for those contractors performing peripheral support operations.

- Withholding payments is a powerful tactic and probably remains the buyer's final resort in pressing for satisfaction. The complexity of any major capital project requires constant discussion between companies and agreed adjustments to the original schedule.

Supply chain management

- Initiated in the Japanese car industry this concept has gained favour rapidly. It has been responsible for moving relationships between supplier and customer away from the normal adversarial situation to a collaborative arrangement. As both parties recognise the stunning savings that can be achieved through the logistical management of supplies, it becomes a mutually advantageous arrangement. Building a longer-term relationship that demands commitment from both parties gives suppliers the opportunity to establish a solid business base.

- In developing this strategy the selection of suppliers becomes of paramount importance. Buying staff need to seek out suppliers who are capable of servicing their short- and medium-term needs. The advice of other functions, particularly technical, and details derived from the customer service assessment provide a firm base for such judgements. A feature is the payment arrangements, with the customer detailing the weekly usage of the supplier's material. This will exclude any supplied product that fails the production performance standards! On receiving these details, the supplier invoices in the normal manner. Payment only for perfect material is a worthy objective.

Unique clauses

The introduction of these clauses is associated with sole supply agreements. It would be unusual for parties to a standard contractual situation to accept such additions.

- *Supplier staff selection.* The customer would approve staff whose input directly affected the well-being of the contract. In circumstances where the personnel are deemed to be unsuitable the supplier would be requested to make the necessary changes. If the supplier, for example, has an excellent trader purchasing his material and any substitute would be unacceptable, the customer may seek to ensure his continued support by making his presence an integral element in the contract.

- *Payment arrangements.* As previously indicated, the customer would advise the supplier of the volumes used and be invoiced accordingly. This allows the customer to ignore reject material and cut down paperwork and removes the previous payment arrangements that included working stock. The timescale for the payment will be the same as for normal deliveries. The agreed time against which payment is made should be enshrined in documents used by both parties to remove the potential for ongoing disagreements.

- *Confidentiality.* Sole supply demands total confidentiality from the supplier's staff and will constrain their direct involvement with other customers, particularly those seen as direct competitors. The confidentiality clause is essential and no working relationship can satisfactorily develop without this clear recognition of inter-dependence.

- *Matching price competition.* All customers will expect the supplier to offer this commitment as an expression of their own confidence. This is a major trade-off between the parties. If the supplier is to gain guaranteed business for a (relatively) long period then the customer will depend on protection in the critical pricing arrangement. 'Never knowingly undersold' is the basis for this exchange.

- *Supply guarantees.* Interruptions in supplies can be difficult and sometimes extremely expensive. The customer will include provisions that cater for such an occurrence. The normal alternatives are: (a) the supplier to obtain material from an 'approved' alternative manufacturer and deliver at the contracted price; or (b) the customer to purchase the items from his own selected alternative manufacturer and request the contracted supplier to pay any additional costs.

The contract is a very important document, hopefully used for regular reference purpose, and will require considerable attention in drafting. *It should receive the most senior commitment from supplier and customer*; this is not paper that is subject to the confirmation of a frontline buyer and salesperson. *It should be written in plain English* to remove as many discrepancies as possible. Business circumstances alter with astonishing rapidity and *the contract needs to be reviewed whenever change is deemed to be significant.*

Buyers should understand the necessity of agreeing contractual terms and ignore the jovial assertion that 'all will be well'.

CHAPTER 8

Lowest cost reduction

Introduction

For the majority of companies that are stretched and challenged in an increasingly competitive market there remains the constant desire to discover a USP (unique sales proposition) that sets them apart and gives them the opportunity for better profit levels. In the event of a corporate USP becoming attractive the urge amongst competitors to mimic may eliminate this differentiation quickly. The ability of companies to match a special feature will depend upon the costs of market entry. To construct a cardboard box manufacturing operation is relatively quick and inexpensive but developing new-generation drugs will demand considerable resources. Much has been written on this subject but, suffice to say, in the absence of a USP the greatest comfort will be derived from an operating base that is very sharp, at a level equal to or below others, so that business may be attracted.

Cost is a very powerful factor – particularly in circumstances where the quality offerings are similar! Economic pressure dictates that least cost products, given parity of quality, will usurp competitors and gain major market shares and volumes. The ancient saw 'to buy well is to sell well' remains absolutely true and lowest cost is an excellent position from which to defend company fortunes.

With any level of supply collaboration the shared objective must be to create options that ensure least cost values.

Stocks

Many supply lines include precautionary just-in-case stocks that reflect a desire to avoid stock outs; for a multiplicity of reasons people act like squirrels and accumulate additional quantities which, inevitably, creates a series of 'extra' reserves. The collective stationery stock held by administration staff always demonstrates the point. If archivists needed to obtain redundant company headed notepaper or purple highlighting pens, a short search of office cupboards would yield an Aladdin's cave!

It is only upon the provision of regular forecasts that, under modern business pressures, serious inroads may be achieved in removing surplus 'back pocket' stocks.

Attitudes are being changed by improved logistics and the universal application of information technology (IT). Gone are the days of grubby handwritten notes as forecasts become credible and better production flows result. The marriage of supply and stock control systems has reduced holding volumes very dramatically, especially at the manufacturing location. The confidence to share forecasts, some of which carry obligations on the provider of the information, has reduced stock levels by more than 60% and created massive additional storage space for finished goods or other supplies, sometimes allowing the closure of overflow storage off-site and improved company cash flow. This early easy success has stimulated the search for further improvements. It demonstrates the absolute power of example.

This is, probably, the first tangible test of collaboration. Neither party has over-committed nor is the information nerve-wrackingly confidential; it may have been provided early but just represents that which would have been provided in the fullness of time. The customer will be sufficiently encouraged by these positive results to envisage raising their commitment and consider longer-term contracts favourably. The joint beneficial activities encourage both parties to expect closer and deeper collaboration.

Product

The establishment of specifications for goods and services purchased entails discussions between internal quality control management, the corporate arbiters, and their counterparts at the supplier. The buyer will seek to obtain the greatest flexibility and may be able to agree specifications that permit substitution. To be granted some freedom of choice will enthuse the buyer and give the company cost advantages. If the interchange of product is allowed by the supply agreement then the buyer may be able to switch between approved materials several times before the actual delivery – and reducing the final invoice cost every time there is a switch! This should be an outstanding opportunity for the buyer to demonstrate market knowledge and skill. Margarine manufacturers have a range of different formulae to satisfy the product performance criteria and, as different oils change in relative price terms, the buyer may switch from one approved specification to another.

The control function of QC management may become distorted and used disadvantageously.

In the dangerous world of new product development (NPD) this is vividly demonstrated when the internal technical staff have, by their own research, identified a supplier, previously unknown to the company, to supply a unique material for their test-kitchen experimentation – and subsequent manufacture! This is not beyond the realms of possibility! (This subject is discussed in Chapter 17.) All purchasing is performed against the required specification agreed between supplier and customer. The latter has the right to reject any material submitted that does not fully comply with the specification. Only in extreme situations does pragmatism override the ruling and, only then, with the consent of the QC personnel. Occasionally the supplies are crucial and may be accepted to prevent factory closures or similar catastrophes!

Purchasing has the responsibility to provide every viable alternative material and/or supplier for consideration. The material may be cheaper and more concentrated, but the objective is to offer alternatives that provide cost savings. Changing suppliers should deliver the same options. Technicians will be required to visit and approve alternative manufacturing locations or changed processes. Their independent clearance is vital.

In developed mature supply relationships the provider of the material should perform the same function. Options are the lifeblood of commercial insurance; when all else has failed, choose another material or supplier! It is a litmus test for a committed supplier if they are willing to offer alternative products in circumstances that will generate lower revenues or profits for themselves.

Pricing

As the prospect of establishing a supply partnership nears, it is critically important that the customer indicates the need for a competition clause that will continue throughout the duration of the contract. It is valid to expect any supplier to meet competition in exchange for the committed business. For the greater level of cooperation, the customer will require protection against the possibility that market prices may move below those agreed in the contract. It is very uncomfortable having a contract that is undermined during the operating period. Nothing destroys confidence more.

In truth, the objective of meeting all levels of competition does allow companies to improve continually upon their internal cost structures. This is a truism for all business operations but the sharing process generates greater opportunities to outperform competition.

No buyer will commit their company's business to long-term contracts without the assurance that intervening factors be included in the terms of supply. In the early discussions for a major contract, in terms of value and timescale, the buyer should declare this condition as essential. The contract will, therefore, contain a John Lewis Partnership style clause (never knowingly undersold) that grants the customer licence to challenge the contract when the market offers pricing that significantly undercuts the agreement level. The longer the contractual term, the greater is the need for such protection.

The customer will increase business in exchange for this surety because it forms the bedrock from which to build.

Comparable price quotations should be regularly obtained to ensure the maintenance of this happy situation. It would be unreasonable to produce ill-founded quotations and expect the partner to immediately adjust their pricing. In circumstances of monopoly, or near-monopoly, supply there may be severe problems in obtaining alternative quotations but this does nothing to detract from the principle. Openness is necessary for this process to add value to the relationship; word of mouth claims should fail so that, in the absence of acceptable and quantifiable evidence, requests for price reductions are ignored. Firm evidence is a prerequisite for this trading condition to be met. It should be understood that price competition must exceed an agreed level before discussions take place; quantifiable prices 5% below the contract level could be seen as an acceptable trigger and it may be ignored if the quote occurs within an agreed period from the commencement of the contract. It is reasonable to expect the contract price to remain inviolate for some time if the buyer has performed well.

This is a forceful stance and will cause anxiety whenever markets change character and move into a mode that ignores profit and is driven by volume considerations only. It is a testing period for both participants and requires pragmatism to chart a course satisfactorily through the temporary turbulence.

Sales and marketing functions are alert to competitive activity for their products and will respond to any adjusted offerings in the market; it is easy to suggest that the buying function is less skilled than the competition!

If a supply partnership has any value it must be based, primarily, on the sound footing that, together, the companies are able to produce a pricing basis capable of being measured against best practice in that industry. This target cannot be achieved without mutual support; the confrontational buying stance has no ability to derive the same benefits through unrefined aggression that survives for long – the supplier will either become bankrupt or dally with other customers, probably competitors!

People

In the process of sharing the responsibilities of those functions forming the interface between companies is the opportunity to reduce (people) overhead costs. The process by which the customer validates the quality of supplied goods and services often replicates the QC procedures performed by the supplier. Satisfying the commonly agreed specification will, therefore, entail some control duplication. In circumstances of shared activity these combined efforts should eliminate some, or all, of the duplication.

Depending upon the level of integration, there should be excellent prospects of sharing or transferring jobs. If the customer has sufficient confidence to expect that the supplier will deliver totally acceptable materials for immediate use there are many potential savings; the QC manager may be better employed on other projects, the warehouseman separating the rejected materials will work elsewhere and the administrative paperwork associated with the returns, credit claims, delayed payments, etc. will become minimal. The ancillary benefits from 'right first time' will be substantial!

Listening to suppliers' advice is difficult but important. Packaging suppliers suffer the indignity of rejected material, for which their engineers, if they had access to the customer's production process, would devise an acceptable solution. The packaging may have a very detailed specification that prevents the use of a wide range of materials, in which case it will offer narrow operating conditions and limited flexibility. Unless the supplier is fully conversant with machine limitations and their engineers have the opportunity of viewing the constraints, much goodwill may evaporate as problems and costs escalate!

Exchange visits between engineers and QC personnel may contribute to further cost-saving opportunities. Supplier engineers will understand the operating conditions for the use of their product; discussions for capital equipment are important and site visits can prevent simple failures. It is disappointing to acknowledge that many suppliers' technicians do not understand the purposes for which their products are required. Too many companies assume that the supplier's technical staff have little or nothing to contribute to an appreciation of their internal processes. Activities may need to be protected and outsiders will be excluded but there may be many instances when a shared knowledge contributes to progress. Blocking out technicians could be self-defeating!

Resource management support

If companies decide that closer collaboration is essential for the growth of their business it provokes the search for opportunities that exist amongst suppliers. The varied character of the supply base dictates that suppliers form a polyglot collection. They produce a wide gamut of goods and services under differing circumstances. Many may be small and lack the financial resources to staff central support functions, so the luxury of enjoying effective advice does not exist. It may, therefore, be determined that, for a brief period, the larger and better financed customer will allow his skilled service managers to be used in identifying improvements in processes and materials so as to generate operational benefits for both parties. Larger corporate customers have freely provided such advice to achieve product cost savings in excess of 20%! That the client company has freed the supplier to offer these benefits to other customers who are potential competitors should be viewed as a side issue in establishing advances. Under most circumstances progress of this nature does not ensure a lengthy advantage in any market – although it would be expected that the supplier continue to provide a competitive edge for a specified timescale.

CHAPTER 9

Open book costing

The trickiest situation that will test both parties to the limit!

Open book costing is an established business principle that will be subject to deep and searching discussions; it is an extremely difficult and hazardous topic. The basis for this procedure is disarmingly straightforward and epitomises an attitude of openness and fulsome cooperation; while this may be reasonable, the buyer should be keenly conscious of the pitfalls involved.

At face value, the principle is undeniably attractive but the complexity encourages misunderstandings that may damage confidence and unwittingly provide suppliers with unjustified protective profit security. Discussions will include lengthy debates about the acceptable level of profit that the supplier should enjoy. These will be an integral element in open book costing and the customer should anticipate these conversations. It is a topic that cannot be avoided and attitudes should be well rehearsed. ·

The relationship between supplier and customer determines the attitudes towards such declarations. The proponents of partnership will promote the activity as an ultimate expression of collaboration, while cynics debunk the activity as spurious and dangerous nonsense.

Open book costing is the 'free' declaration of supplier costs and profitability that support their invoices for goods and services. It is intended to be a full disclosure of internal component costs and, handled appropriately, it can identify opportunities for mutual gain. The companies will establish a base from which future price applications may be assessed and, given the prior exhaustive examinations to confirm the starting values, it is probable that the price changes will receive easy approval. It is also likely that price changes will move at a pace determined by the applicant. Little imagination is needed to compare this near-automatic change procedure with those in open market circumstances and, inevitably, the declaration of pre-priced commitments, on which there will be exaggerated profits, may be misleading! Caveat emptor.

Additionally, if mishandled and misunderstood, it may conceal inefficiencies and add to product costs through the sanction of the client; each company may have different but legitimate interpretations of the incremental summary. The different financial procedures alone may expose the alternative approaches that preclude any confident joint assessments being made.

Open book costing is valueless for buyers who pursue a free-market stance that rejects any suggestion of closer relationship with their suppliers. They prefer the hard, often uneconomic, world of competitive bidding that ignores the supplier's need for profit. Logically this stance delivers improved cost control at the supplier and may match the alternative collaborative process. Hard unyielding customers, if their business is wanted, will forcibly move the supplier into a more competitive position from which it may profit considerably. If suppliers are determined to stay the course and capture the desired business, the process of natural selection may result in their position improving, as the less combative companies will have died. In many markets this natural struggle for economic survival is epitomised by the weakest disappearing to be replaced by other companies ready to compete for volume on the basis of almost non-existent margins. Markets that reflect such insensitivity are providing low-specification goods from innumerable suppliers. They will be characterised by producers with short life expectations and are driven by tactical expediency rather than any strategic considerations. Most buying shows little or no interest in cost profiles or profit levels because, in the event of supply failure, there are certain to be abundant alternative sources.

To entertain open book costing, the buyer and his/her colleagues must have access to a wide range of skills, namely good market knowledge, an understanding of production procedures, financial advice and an understanding of the supplier's purchasing strategies. The support of financial advisers is crucial in the analysis. To attempt otherwise is foolhardy because it may move purchasing into sanctioning imperfections and, worse, will not replicate the inevitable market pressure to improve. It is naive to assume that buying will have sufficient expertise to prevent the loss of market advantage.

If, however, the buyer needs any element of assistance or collaboration from their chosen supplier, open book costing will become an issue! If the supplier possesses an unknown advantage that is translated into the invoiced pricing, this process can provide an opportunity to assess the basis for such benefits and, naturally, a chance to renegotiate. For instance, constructing a cost profile for flavours and colours based on a common carrier such as salt will produce substantial savings. Similarly, the UK cheese manufacturing industry is based on the use of starter mediums derived from chemical formulae that were jealously protected by producers. There are substantial development costs as technicians build effective unique products, in a similar manner to the pharmaceutical industry(!). However, through constructing a cost profile incorporating the quoted costs of production and the base carrier it was possible to convince the supplier of the need for a major reduction in pricing. It truncates the high margins that are used to recover the development costs.

Open book costing, properly administered, does expose opportunities to improve that may, otherwise, remain hidden. It has the distinct advantage of providing the client with an overview from which, with the support of their internal skills, they may gain substantially. To use experienced managers as proactive consultants, through visits, who can identify process improvements is an extremely powerful tool. This suggests that this programme will be attractive to larger customers able to support such programmes. If the client is small in comparison with their supplier, it requires considerable care.

The examination of purchasing procedures and strategies at the supplier are debated elsewhere (see Chapters 5 and 2) but open book costing can be valuable if organised with full agreement between parties. It should, however, never be entertained if collaboration is less than wholehearted. Too many suppliers have benefited from the simplistic notion that open book costing is a declaration of honest intent while, unfortunately, being an approval system that prevents natural market pressures from driving change. Preserving inefficiencies should not appeal!

Recent academic suggestions that the open book procedure is subject to misrepresentation may have some validity so buyers should ensure that any analyses of proffered cost profiles are subjected to close scrutiny by their internal financial function. To perform the assessment using untrained staff is irresponsible.

The purchasing function must anticipate being challenged to exercise choice in favour of this costing system. It will become more obvious as the relationship builds and interdependency increases. Preparedness is vital and an early declaration as to the attitude and benefits that can be derived from this procedure is needed. If there is a presumption that, together, the companies will produce a fully competitive situation by mutual support, open book costing will possess considerable advantages. It forges the relationship and draws the participants inextricably closer. In the event of separation, the customer will retain, for the short and medium period, a valuable database from which to perform evaluations of alternative suppliers more effectively than in the past. Market knowledge is powerful and creating a measurement framework is invaluable.

Open book costing has immense value in situations that produce two or more cost profiles for the same, or similar, products. Cross-comparison makes analysis very easy.

This popular procedure has the opportunity of building a collective least-cost programme of individual projects. Rolls Royce supported a small component supplier who found meeting the latest RR request for *more* reductions in costs beyond their abilities. Rolls Royce extended their operational support freely so that, over a short time, the supplier's manufacturing cost profile fell by 15% and, in consequence, they were able to meet the target. Depending on the strategic importance of the supplier, most customers would be keen to perform similar 'consultative' actions. It is mutually satisfying and becomes valuable when the partnership has sufficient confidence for one company to declare a difficulty. Open book costing should never be viewed as a profit guarantee but as an opportunity for both parties to examine and, together, improve performances.

No business relationship, of any worth, will be sustained without challenges generated by either partner. Progress is made from constructive criticism and confidence.

CHAPTER 10

Communications: electronic and otherwise

Introduction

The entertaining game of Chinese Whispers graphically demonstrates misunderstandings that poor communications can provide; when 'send reinforcements we're going to advance' can be translated into 'send three-and-four pence we're going to a dance' there is no doubt that considerable anxiety can be generated by similar uncontrolled messages passing between companies.

Communications is a subject on which everyone has an opinion, and as it is usually at odds with everyone else, the surety, therefore, is that misunderstandings will continue. A mixture of lack of thought, time pressures and proxy messengers may place emphases that were not intended. To compound these circumstances by adding language misunderstandings is to increase the likelihood of mistakes. Retrieving the errors is time-consuming and expensive.

Giving the correct message

It is desirable to be assured that the process is foolproof from the outset! Wherever possible, the initiators of messages, orders, commands and information should also be the messengers and, given the easy access to electronic mail systems, this is possible. The plethora of desktop PCs and the associated removal of secretarial support make this a credible option. Managers, today, are computer-friendly and can issue clear messages. The capability of being able to visually check the intended information gives the originator an invaluable opportunity to remove uncertainties.

The messages exchanged between companies should be carefully checked and incapable of being misunderstood. It is very important that the 'sponsoring' function has the ability to view all communications; purchasing should have sight of the most salient correspondence until sufficient experience has been accumulated to determine the level at which the banal becomes important. While this may appear excessively heavy-handed, the maintenance of good working relationships is critical and purchasing is responsible for ensuring delivery of the commercial benefits.

The simplest communication comprises orders for goods and services that is often a telephoned request followed by posted hard-copy documents to confirm. In almost every instance this is the direct repetition of factual details, volumes, price, date and time of delivery, etc. Every other message is complex, open to misinterpretation and managed by several different functions in both companies! The KISS (keep it simple, stupid!) principle has much to commend it; the regular information flow needs careful analysis, together with an agreed activity schedule to support any temporary operators, e.g. holiday relief.

The role for computers

The universal availability of computer-based systems has pressed businesses to adapt their administration and gain the cost benefits. Two-way information transfer is common practice and allows continuous supervision. An order and delivery requirement is a simple process that has, historically, been submerged by paperwork and subject to many different control procedures.

It is very important to acknowledge the management function performed by purchasing in resolving any operational difficulties. Purchasing must oversee the building of links, resolve the arguments and channel energies positively so that internal perceptions remain supportive for further extensions. Innocent or Machiavellian misuse of inter-company channels of communication will cause trouble so that boringly competent practices need constant reiteration. *Shared responsibilities make for confusion and mutual recrimination.*

The Internet: selecting the appropriate uses

The modern electronic world is beguiling and powerful. Fertile 'nerd' brains are constructing programs and systems at such an amazing pace that today's inventions become redundant tomorrow. Associated marketing hype can damage the perception of business leaders. It attempts to persuade potential customers that implementation delivers astounding benefits and counsels that acceptance by competitors will lead to hellfire, loss of market share and damnation! In response, however, business has been cautious and slow to embrace the new communication options.

Early market disasters for embryo Internet businesses have signalled the completion of the first phase of experimentation towards establishing e-mail as a future contact medium. The powerful hype has been characterised by an explosion of websites, primarily developed by marketing and sales functions, many of which have problems caused by speedy installation without linked support systems. Any resultant stock outs are commercial disasters. Reviewers suggest that corporate management rejected sound business judgement by rushing into ecommerce and have fallen prey to their own enthusiasm. The imagined urgency to stay on the 'cutting edge' has damaged perceptions and given comfort to the reticent followers; trail blazing is a fraught role!

Innovation generates extreme reactions and Internet trading is the latest fashion; buyers expect any e-mail program to be a precursor to gaining price benefits. If the screen provides market information, the conclusion is for improved terms to result; otherwise there is little to be gained from a soulless machine! Sellers, however, visualise the process as extending their marketplace exponentially and creating the opportunity of managing customer requirements into reduced product ranges. This provides mixed messages and confusion that, coupled with operational problems, is dissuading customers from launching themselves into the future mode of communication.

Internet programs are demonstrating two major benefits for all buying staff: the provision of additional information in a format that facilitates comparisons and massive cost savings on order processing. Buyers need information; it is their lifeblood, and any method of supporting and assisting intelligent decisions will be welcome. To buy goods or materials from a market that is unfamiliar is challenging; the Internet has the capacity to yield considerable informational data on supplier products, general pricing, availability, etc., that contribute to better buying decisions.

Administration cost savings

The electronic transfer of administrative documentation (orders, despatch details and invoices) is yielding significant cost reductions in processing. In comparison with historical purchase order formats, the present costs represent 10% of previous levels and will, as the procedures become more sophisticated, deliver greater gains. This will improve labour utilisation and facilitate staff allocation to either alternative effective work or redundancy. Electronic data interchange (EDI) has spawned many programs that replace existing practices.

The universal acceptance of electronic mail, especially documents confirming inter-company business, is challenging auditors to accept signatures, attached to fax, e-mail documents, etc. as valid.

Administration cost penalties

There are negative aspects of the electronic revolution and it is necessary to highlight a serious unexpected disadvantage associated with PC-driven processes. Many studies continue to confirm the continued proliferation of paper even after the installation of computer procedures. The battle against paper mountains shows no sign of being won; in fact there is strong evidence that the opposite effect has occurred. It appears that the paperless office remains a dream and that, ignoring innumerable government initiatives, the regulatory machine demands continue to increase. The love affair with hard copy is difficult to shift. A recent study by Lexmark, computer printer manufacturers bears witness to the human need for hard copy versions of PC data.

Security concerns are creating cautious business attitudes towards adopting Internet systems. High profile cases of 'hacking' into government systems, assumed foolproof, have provided sufficient justification for this reticence. The thought that corporate strategies, product launches and executive bonus structures could become widespread public knowledge causes panic! Current attitudes suggest that casual mistakes by staff members, added to their general sense of security, provoke serious failures. Creation of firewalls and use of anti-virus components are essential pre-conditions to encourage greater acceptance. It is apparent that company management is being pressed to adopt the electronic operating systems as reduced staffing levels become a reality.

Companies should install communication methodology, which, if well managed, will accelerate understanding, and, in tandem, speedily remove areas of misunderstanding. This process must be managed carefully because early experience shows that employees, empowered to send messages through the Internet, generated 85% 'junk' messages through their enthusiastic espousal! It is an activity that may cause serious misuse because of the natural temptation to send personal messages that have no relevance to the business. Indeed, in a world of lengthy working days, there is a significant proportion of employees who find playing PC-based games more challenging than their job responsibilities.

Failures

General management has been negligent by distancing itself from the development and testing of computer programs. Much money and acrimony has been spent on inappropriate systems that fail to deliver the expected results. Examples abound that serve to indict CEOs for their assumption that IT managers fully understand the corporate requirements for all computer programs. For several years, senior managers have decided that their company requires an IT function that builds an electronic infrastructure to support the business. There has, subsequently, been no active management of projects by general management for whom the systems would operate and the IT specialists have effectively built to their own specification. It is foolish to assume that gifted IT program designers have knowledge of the general business world while the manner in which data is requested by senior managers indicate(s) IT illiteracy!

The cost consequences associated with this error are mind-blowing. Rarely are new computer programs delivered on time, within budget and operational. Problems abound and reflect the corporate inability to voice the precise requirements of management and mesh these aspirations with IT designers who *are* able to understand. Regular progress checking allows continual re-evaluation and reassurance.

It is easy to follow the corporate desire to have an 'off-the-shelf' computer program for speed and cost; it is also clear that inadequate consultations have taken place during the development schedule and that glib optimistic time commitments have forced the pace for installation. These factors provide general explanations for delays and failed systems that do *not* yield the expected results for management to use. Massive care is required to control the program to deliver the expectations.

Extending this process into the inter-company communications arena tempts similar fates and, therefore, demands exhaustive checks, trials and balances throughout the development process. The shared prize is major cost reductions and the fast transfer of information, which allows greater stock management, lower stock levels and efficient production procedures. To make haste slowly is advice that deserves repetition. The incompatibility of differing computer software programs has become a historical blemish. Although connecting arrangements are needed, there is little or no obstacle to the interlinking of computers. No business can ignore this new methodology and, should the system be rejected, the reasoning needs regular revisiting. The target should be reduced time, reduced costs in manpower and administrative processes and reduced paper. If these advances are achieved, the business is well positioned. There is no dishonour in moving carefully and mimicking the antics of the pioneers. It is sufficient, however, to record the massive cost benefits of constructing electronic communication programs that remove as many manual procedures as possible.

Face to face

Regular activity reviews should involve executive representatives from both companies; too often, once the early glamour has diminished, the leading managers transfer their responsibilities to a designated subordinate and immediately throw the conversations into an ineffective 'talking shop'. While this change is understandable, clear directives and a readiness to attend those meetings requiring decisions must accompany it. The meetings may be unexciting, lacking the drama of a full-blown scare, but are important none the less. Confidence-building between companies may fail to inspire many functions whose time is precious and who have to delegate their support to an ineffective staff member. Sufficient executive power should be invested in this process so that each meeting enjoys total corporate attention. The importance of such reviews is to prevent an outbreak of war! To build reputations takes much longer than the brief period that can destroy a liaison.

Purchasing is expected to manage the various channels to ensure continuous progress and early resolution of problems. This activity is unglamorous and attracts ennui. It is a hard road to tread.

CHAPTER 11

Electronic systems: e-mail and all that!

Introduction

The painstaking work performed by medieval monks in producing their amazing illustrated books has been followed by successive waves of innovation. Printing presses, typewriters, and microfiche improved methods of recording and communicating. The computer is the latest development to promote great change and is revolutionising our working patterns. Combining technology and telecommunications broadens the potential exponentially and the Internet explosion is the latest fashion for business to understand and develop.

As business reassembles the broken pieces of the initial Internet revolution and restores some confidence, the early mistakes are guiding second-generation participants. Dotcoms spent heavily in building a brand presence, almost from zero, but customer service and satisfaction were low-key objectives. Legal risk management was ignored.

Management caution

Experience has caused senior management to tread carefully into the computer world; this activity has suffered bad press with several high-profile failures. It has been late (technology has moved further forward), ineffective (it has not fulfilled the original specified needs, either through bad design or incorrect briefing) and expensive (substantially beyond the budget)! The early Gadarene-like rush has subsided and progress will be made steadily – with caution and circumspection.

Most companies are uncertain about the construction of bespoke programs for their use and are more confident, therefore, in accepting standard equipment and systems that have successfully been tested by others. Pioneers seem to get shot very quickly!

The market is awash with too many unsubstantiated claims. It is suggested, without foundation, that this new technology (information and communications) enables faster economic growth without raising inflation. There is no evidence that the large increase in IT investment has raised the rate of productivity yet. Corporate capital expenditure has supported Internet programmes by altering investment priorities and switching money away from other projects. Many companies, persuaded to capture the massive cost benefits, have discovered the exhausting demands on managers and employees. When Royal & Sun Alliance, the multinational insurance company, introduced a procurement system in only 14 weeks, involving 16,000 staff, it found the process surprisingly difficult. While the software proved satisfactory, the project involved 70 full-time employees, was expensive to install, too sophisticated for some suppliers and could be justified in terms of the cost of the investment only by expanding the procurement categories on the system.

What is uncontested is the ease of communication; the process is very fast and personalised and the transfer of information (orders etc.) to several contacts simultaneously potentially removes hard copies. Industry is 'feeling its way' through the security concerns and will create firewall arrangements to equal those features in operation elsewhere.

Purchasing will enjoy major advantages, some obvious and operating today and others yet to be discovered.

For companies intent upon streamlining the supply chain and using this modern technology, the adoption of e-procurement is an early decision. This methodology possesses linked programmes from which companies may obtain additional benefits. The purchasing of maintenance, repair and operations (MRO) fits neatly and, depending on the guaranteed service levels, internal stocks may be reduced almost to zero. Office stationery can be decimated. The initial change in procedure often results in no direct orders as the company first works its way through the six months of stock heaped in filing cabinets!

Operating benefits

Much administration work, in time and paper, can be mechanised so that buying staff will be released to concentrate on exercising their skills. It is estimated that manual systems occupy 70% of a buyer's day and the United Nations has estimated that 7% of international trade is swallowed up each year by the cost of administering paper-based systems. The tangible benefits lie in cutting the administration paper chase. The mechanisation of purchase order processing has lowered the cost for each order and shortened the time between order and delivery. Advocates of e-procurement claim that the cost of an order has been reduced by a factor of ten. It has become a universal panacea.

Electronic contact between supplier and customer has become standard practice so that, in advanced circumstances, suppliers are able to examine, automatically, stock levels held at their customers' sites and perform a replenishment programme independently. The transfer of automatic measurements direct to the supply source removes any element of manual misreporting. BOC (British Oxygen Company) and Air Products used to provide storage tanks for customers to hold industrial gases and the stock control system operated in this fashion.

It is encouraging that this efficient procedure has been reinvented. The provision of on-line catalogues from which internal customers may order replenishments completes the transfer of business management to the supplier who will invoice on an agreed timescale. This sequential interlocking process should be carefully managed to prevent an expensive partner becoming so entrenched that extracting your company from their embrace is difficult and expensive. To accept the astonishing benefits requires both a clear recognition of the attendant risks and careful planning.

EDI and similar systems have persuaded auditors of the control system's effectiveness so that automatic direct order requisition transfer is approved and established. The person initiating the order may, using a screen-based form, complete the details and despatch it directly to the supplier. The computer program has sufficient control procedures to prevent abuse. In a company with multiple order sites/people the controls should include personal expenditure limits and each request will be recorded for regular management reviews. This procedure includes a single computerised request form with the single-entry details being retained throughout the administrative process, thus eliminating any incorrect transfer that results in the wrong material or services being delivered. The dependency on reliable input increases.

Businesses have incorporated e-mail for order and information transfer but cautiously approached the alternative options being touted by the proponents of the Internet. Having watched the demise of early entries, it is much like the tale concerning the hare and the tortoise! Caution is drawing purchasing along the road of testing and teasing the new range of options now available. In constructing the early forms of e-procurement, companies have a clear understanding of the range of non-purchasing functions that are responsible for expenditure. The process of empowering individuals to purchase during the introduction of corporate cards was instructive and e-procurement replicates this discovery.

The realisation is healthy because of the executive decisions that are invoked: should purchasing control all expenditure? If not why not, and what control levels should be exercised upon each individual allowed to purchase on behalf of the company?

Reviewing procedures

Examining procedures and existing expenditure is stunningly effective and promotes excellent savings. Regular challenges arise from the multiple approval signatures required to purchase standard cheap equipment, the relative high cost of raising orders for an item of very low value and the aggregation of orders that elevate the value into a serious issue deserving some research rather than the unthinking routine ordering! Knowledge is all-powerful!

The Internet as a source of information

Buying opportunities devolve from the process of gathering information and the Internet is an excellent source. The value of this knowledge depends upon the extent of the database and regular maintenance of each company site. Searching for potential new suppliers should be easy. The trend towards supplier rationalisation may be reversed in selective sectors; buying paper clips may not be critical in any measure and the incentive to search worldwide is strong. Theoretically this newest electronic marketplace should provide sufficient options to satisfy the most demanding buyer. However, in each instance where the buyer wishes to discuss pricing there is a constraint; buyers will determine those goods and services for which they want to create an individual agreement. Under these circumstances it is unlikely that an electronic system will perform any critical function.

There are several Internet trading exchanges being formed that offer the opportunity to buy market goods and the arrangement may attract those companies needing a swift, inexpensive process to order low-value items. It may spawn the familiar individual discounts from published price lists. Buyers remain conservative about this new technology and are examining a range of options. The provision of Internet information, including product details and a list price, leading to direct negotiation, may illustrate the next phase. Selling organisations have stepped towards this solution by including a screen-based trigger to begin an electronic exchange. However, the complexity of the buyer–seller relationship still presents challenges. An American trader of fresh produce commented, 'you've got to talk to people and say when you will pick up the fruit, talk about the variety or label. The actual negotiations cannot be stripped down to screen play!'

Summary

Administration and communications are obvious beneficiaries by speed and cost, whereas improving on invoice payments is less obvious. In building a cluster of programmes to manage this activity range, there are lock-on additions that extend into production planning and forecasting. The cumulative benefits are impressive but the creation of purchasing opportunities is more uncertain and will need further experimentation.

CHAPTER 12

Engineers and boffins

Introduction

Managing external suppliers is a two-fold exercise in which purchasing performs a catalytic role. The buying team coordinates the inter-company dialogue and has, therefore, as much responsibility for the internal functions involved as it does for those of the supplier. Facing both ways doubles this load and managing company colleagues can be a challenge. This is partly because everybody believes that they understand buying, partly because they believe that their specialist knowledge permits them to exercise judgements that 'stray' into the buying arena and partly because they believe they possess an innate privilege within their discipline that allows them to purchase equipment that they have been charged to obtain.

Whatever the reasoning, there remains the ticklish problem of working closely with functions and 'persuading' them to adapt their role to the company advantage because of your buying skills. There is never an easy method that guarantees success, but you must overcome all obstacles for serious commercial reasons.

Be mindful

Often innocence, and a desire to assist, creates disastrous situations. A young marketing manager, wishing to launch a new product, requests the technical department to obtain sample components for preliminary testing. The technician provides the samples and gives an indication of the price that had been given by the supply salesman. Aghast at the high cost quoted, the marketer withdraws the project, only to see a major competitor establish valuable business for their equivalent product that matches his original projections exactly, including prices! The whole episode is a salutary illustration of total failure.

It is, unfortunately, not isolated because technicians are regularly given a brief from marketing to search the world. They anxiously trawl through massive reference books – the Internet databases – to select potential suppliers based in deepest Siberia who have never supplied the company and, before the buyers can rein in their enthusiasm, have obtained samples at price levels that defy belief.

Or there is the company engineer who has worked assiduously with selected machinery suppliers, chosen by his department, and, on the basis of trials, expresses an unequivocal preference for a particular machine and blithely accepts the proffered price structure. Unwinding deals is difficult, often impossible and assuredly tarnishes external business relationships.

These examples suggest the extraordinary effort required to escape the economic consequences. The purchasing function should discuss responsibilities, impress other functions with their commercial prowess and manage the information flow. They should agree preferred supplier accreditation with technical functions and request that alternative products offered by visiting technical salesmen be advised to the purchasing function for consideration and action. For the engineers the solution is signally different and involves purchasing being able to restrain its narrow enthusiasm for one supplier and maintain a discreet silence until the commercial parameters have been established. Shared meetings with potential suppliers should be encouraged because it prevents any misunderstandings developing. Of particular importance is the creation of penalty clauses that are agreed between purchasing and the engineering functions. The manner in which penalties are to be implemented is crucial.

We all recognise the eminent hospital specialist who has trodden the corridors as a Colossus and is given total respect! Herein lies the insuperable obstacle to effective buying. The specialist sees salespeople, dictates his or her selection and the purchase proceeds at full price. There has been no discussion, internal or otherwise, about alternative products or managing the purchase of the selected equipment to obtain best value and the buying manager has the fraught problem of recovering the price premium from unrewarding purchases of paper towels, office stationery and cleaning fluids! This is a scenario that, unfortunately, continues to haunt many hospital groups today. The solution is too obvious to encourage any lengthy debate because the attendant cost is beyond contemplation! Buying is a cost upon the health sector, performed by those well hidden from view and whose credibility is zero. All that is left is for the purchasing manager to persuade hospital management to trial the alternative procedure – any alternative procedure – and measure the results. Acorns and oak trees!

It would be reassuring to imagine that these illustrations are unusual, in the past and merely amusing. *Not so!* They replicate themselves with monotonous certainty. The examples contain sufficient detail to permit one to guess at the corporate losses!

Be careful

Buyers have to persuade every function of their value. The role is total communication and building an internal network into which buyers can feed. It is very important to be proactive and warn the company of, for example, supply problems or major price changes. It is a restless responsibility and never disappears!

Purchasing must, conversely, suck details from the company for efficient supply management. The suppliers are heavily dependent upon information and this will emerge in different guises; marketing may be considering a new pack size for which the supplier does not have the appropriate packing configuration, production is attempting to use returnable plastic pallets and finance are installing a new payment system that requires the invoices to be presented in a different layout. Lack of timely advice causes serious complications, all of which will carry an inherent cost. Industry remains in a supplicant attitude as these simple unquantifiable cost penalties are borne without complaint! Imagine, therefore, the pleasure derived from successfully managing an administrative change with all parties knowledgeable and involved!

Be proactive

Selling the function is vital. Invest time and a little money in making contacts, friends and supporters. Publicise your successes, issue eye-catching leaflets trumpeting your role, and push yourself forward as an important key to corporate success. Try desperately hard to avoid being managed by the finance department because they lack imagination, are risk-averse and cannot think beyond last week's profit and loss statements. Be shy of being subsumed by production for the agenda that forces an entirely different set of objectives on you; delivery on time every time is second only to the cry that all suppliers have failed to produce packaging capable of running efficiently on the machines. Try to be your own person and, while direct reporting may be beyond your capabilities, find a function (marketing?) who have no direct operational contact but are able to recognise your skills and contributions and possess the innate abilities to press your suit at the higher exalted levels!

Fanciful? Perhaps, but the position of purchasing is important for the public profile it enjoys and the opportunity to impress.

CHAPTER 13

The immovable supplier

Introduction

Not every supplier is an amicable friend just hoping for business on your terms! There will be suppliers who, for various reasons, are impervious to your greatest efforts and remain unmoved and stony-faced. Some tactics may provide a little light relief but it is foolish to suggest that a universal panacea exists.

The following examples illustrate gambits that may succeed but the essential tactic is to attempt the unexpected. Lateral thinking is helpful, as is planning a stepped progression in your approach, because any instant collapse of the 'stout party' is unlikely. However, try, try and try again. Change your approach, attempt the unusual or unexpected; appeal for help and call in the seventh cavalry!

The advice is to establish a priority action plan that concentrates energy on the options most likely to yield progress. Although no one wishes to concede failure, it is foolish to chase the impossible target.

The representative

Company relationships are influenced by the rapport between buyer and seller; the personal chemistry is a major factor and can yield extra advantages that are delivered without any additional cost. Bookshelves are full of erudite advisory tomes concerning interpersonal skills – so these suggestions are intended to break a perceived logjam for your benefit.

Regardless of the interpersonal relationship, if there is no progress, the most obvious tactic is to complain to the supplier about their representative. Any vague justification is acceptable; it is, after all, obvious that you are not gaining any commercial benefit and time is slipping away. Another face on the other side of the table may produce the thaw you seek.

Change your behaviour, become unpredictable, threaten loudly if you are usually quiet and reserved, invite spectators – playing a role – to record the conversations and 'pressurise' the visitor. Request that a senior manager replaces the representative because decisions are not being made under the present arrangement. Anything to disrupt the balance!

The monopoly supplier

This company is a common feature of markets where the economic 'entry' costs are very high, where patent protection remains, and which is characterised by those who, clearly, know of their special value to you, partly because your colleagues have openly complimented them on that fact.

Blandishments fall on deaf ears, the cost profiles of patented materials are not available and direct threats carry no value! Government legislation is destroying any pretence at secrecy; the law requires manufacturers to give fuller disclosure than previously so that, perhaps emboldened with confidentiality agreements, your technical staff may visit the supplier's production site and construct an assessment of the product cost profile. Unique materials are, commonly, created from a mix of basic ingredients, the cost of which will be easily established. This process will create a theoretical pricing for the 'special' unknown materials. As the prices for the basic materials change, it provides an opportunity to raise the cost issues. The supplier recognises your intelligence and may begin to respond; *the initial discussion will have a greater impact if it follows a market price reduction.* Life may not be sufficiently compliant! This attempt will hinge greatly upon your company's technical expertise.

Concentrate on the indirect cost elements that do not appear on the invoice! Persistently discussing every detail will, with skill and persistence, construct an invaluable databank. The most productive opportunities usually relate to the services performed by the supplier: deliveries, payment arrangements and alternative specifications. If there are opportunities to demonstrate that the service or delivery is less than perfect, they should be taken avidly, it transfers the advantage, albeit temporarily, to you. From every chink there comes light. Select an option that separates the 'mainstream' debate away from the 'expected' price contest and seize any opportunity to complain. Monopoly suppliers develop a justified arrogance and are discomfited by suggestions of imperfect service. Badly stacked pallets, broken pallets, late deliveries and incorrect paperwork will provide the opportunity to seek the Achilles heel! If substantiated, these blemishes should 'carry' a financial conse-quence for which your company will require recompense. Game on!

Seek other approaches that will yield some price benefit and raise your standing in their estimation. Stress the interest in joint 'developments', with your company performing the 'guinea pig' role. The supplier will attempt to retain their pre-eminence but providing a test bed for their experimental prototypes, if acceptable to your production management, will achieve multiple benefits, including preferred customer status. This could alter the relationship immeasurably.

Tetrapak is a most successful international supplier of production machinery *and* the associated packaging. Everyone will have drunk liquids from their cartons. The frequency with which their machines and cartons intertwine perfectly shows complete alignment. Customers using this arrangement have the reassurance that, in the event of failure, only one supplier is involved and, importantly, the machines should fill the cartons successfully. This is a situation that delivers exceedingly good returns for Tetrapak.

To import alternative cheaper cartons requires substantial support from production engineers whose paramount concern is with machine efficiencies. To tamper with a smooth operation needs great persuasion and sound financial incentives. A leading UK milk producer believed that, to obtain any useful commercial concessions from Tetrapak, would involve showing a determination to countenance alternative carton suppliers. It would require cost profiling the carton, changing the supply procedures and committing volumes. A European Union directive that separated the machines from the carton supply to encourage competition aided the strategy. This gave customers some intangible advantage, the moral high ground, and the investigation, into market dominance, handed the buyers considerable strength. Over a two-year period this achieved a reduction of 28% in the direct carton costs. In addition the supplier paid for supply inefficiencies and reduced outstanding stock balances significantly. Strangely, the business relationship improved markedly and innovative packaging designs were offered to this customer before any other market competitor.

Sometimes, of course, you may have created a monopolistic situation, in that the commercial benefits and technological advantages may have persuaded your company to invest in a one-on-one arrangement. There will have been considerable debate before this situation became established and the rationale will need regular revision as markets change. Any monopoly agreement is speedily recognised by other potential suppliers and sharp enthusiastic quotations will disappear. It may preclude access to market information and become uncomfortable if a viable alternative supply source arises. Major currency swings, determined investment plans in this market from new manufacturers or loss of key personnel at the present supplier could produce these circumstances *and you would like to escape!*

The unease expressed by other internal functions with total reliance on one source will surface spontaneously and accusing fingers begin to point in the direction of buying. It therefore behoves the function to determine alternative action plans in the event of major disruptions with the supplier. The latter should demonstrate their disaster recovery plan which will be expected to satisfy internal colleagues. The plan may involve different production processes or components and the agreement should be certain.

Sometimes there are no simple failsafe arrangements and, in these situations, expensive alternatives become the norm. The buyer faces creating strategic stocks, paying premium prices for supply certainty and performing wriggling acquiescence to the supplier's payment terms. It is an unappealing option and every buyer will struggle mightily to avoid it.

Whenever a company is heavily dependent upon unique supplies, it is important to provoke other suppliers in an effort to raise their interest in becoming a second source. They would expect their investment to be supported by a firm contract commitment which, naturally, is conditional on the new supplier meeting your material specifications. This scenario is unusual but could construct successful partnerships out of an unpropitious situation.

The arrogant supplier without whom you cannot exist

We meet the master race! These suppliers can be seriously challenged by a determined concentration on service. Failing to achieve perfect delivery will cause psychological mayhem; the early rebuff will be replaced by allegations of malpractice on your part. It should, however, be possible to create, with or without compliance, a systematic check that supports financial claims for operational inconvenience. The current philosophical fashion of right-first-time should provide good material for discussion. Under these circumstances the existing representative is not appropriate for serious discussions and a senior manager is needed to resolve this serious situation.

This will allow you to choose, carefully, the contact with whom to discuss matters of import. Their representative quickly loses credence and confidence if you 'buck' their contact structure and establish understanding with their immediate superiors.

Should you possess any additional business to tempt them with, it is of inestimable value. There should be no extra business without concessions on the existing trade, prices, specifications, etc. This is straightforward and obvious, but timing is critical. Disclose your hand too early and damage ensues, but the eleventh-hour game has much to be admired!

The UK government is a major user of automated office machinery, including photocopiers, and the importance of this business was sufficient for Rank Xerox to have a representative specially assigned to the account. Considerable attention was given to all enquiries and requirements.

Within the Foreign & Commonwealth Office the photocopier contract was a salesman's delight and, effectively, excluded competition from gaining easy access. At regular intervals the photocopier contract would be open to tender. In 1998 the tender was in an advanced stage. With Rank Xerox confidently anticipating the renewal, the sense of aggrievement became overwhelming for a senior FCO manager... and the game began! The new objectives became (a) seamless supply to internal customers at competitive prices using machinery that was technically up to date; (b) adjusting the number of machines without any penalty during the contract period; and (c) allowing the FCO to test alternative machines during this timescale.

The prospect of losing the contract, aided and abetted by law suits, caused major disruption at Rank Xerox. The salesman was undermined, FCO senior management, aware of the tactical plan, ignored his pleas and, although Rank Xerox enjoy the new contract, substantial inroads were made in the pricing. The FCO now has the ability to challenge cost throughout the contract term. They also obtained outstanding terms on machine flexibility and replacement strategy and their success led other government departments to improved supply arrangements. Gone was the 'watch this easy account crumble and we'll keep another captive customer' attitude and the relationship moved into better balance.

CHAPTER 14

Stock management systems

Introduction

Under circumstances in which the supplier and customer have decided that coordinated action will yield mutual benefits, exhaustive planning and communication are vital. This prevents misunderstanding and persuades other corporate functions of the advantages to be gained from collaboration. The pressures and pace of modern business contain so many inherent hazards that identifying shared benefits should be carefully and methodically measured rather than pursued in a frantic and thoughtless manner. The perceived advantages of hasty actions may seem attractive but they could create lukewarm support or, sometimes, outright hostility.

The impetus is the recognition of attractive shared benefits that result from working together; the customer is committed to providing their forecasted requirements in exchange for the reduced stocks held in their warehouse and at the supplier, because the latter is able to improve their production scheduling. There will be many additional factors on which further progress can be made to deliver savings and underline the developing relationship.

The companies should test progress and debate the extent to which they wish to explore this path further. The ultimate goal may be a relationship that companies might find claustrophobic; progress sees a greater level of sharing internal information and will be interpreted by other market participants as an exclusive arrangement. The enthusiastic and aggressive offers will drift away to seek a more welcoming target.

The first stage

The easiest and most productive step is to supply materials based on a firm requirement for future delivery that contains a greater level of certainty than ever before! In exchange, the supplier improves the supply service that enables the customer's stockholding to be reduced. A characteristic symptom is the increased number of deliveries that are performed by part-loads without any recognisable cost additions!

The substantial first stock reduction in the customer's warehouse is impressive but, financially, has only a single impact upon cash flow. So amazing is the stock shrinkage that elation needs restraint, where FMCG (fast moving consumer goods) warehouse stocks falling to 40% of previous levels have been the norm. While it may be easy to overstate the ease with which lower stocks are managed, there is little doubt that embarrassing discoveries of 'old' outdated stocks are less likely to happen. This major shift occurs so quickly that unfettered enthusiasm needs to be restrained because further improvements are dependent upon more complex issues.

Before the stock control programme commences there are essential features to be agreed between parties. Changes in market demand will cause the customer to (a) have the comfort of a minimum stock available that guarantees continuity whenever the demand increases *but* (b) avoid the need for stock commitments beyond which they cannot see business!

Every business is anxious to avoid stock write-off problems in holding surplus stock that has a book value but *no* market value. This contrasts with the supplier who will be keen to receive firm demands for a period as far forward as possible to ensure efficient production. The companies will seek a compromise position for these irreconcilable desires so that, as experience is gained, the agreed circumstances may be adjusted. It is an absolute prerequisite that each partner understands the operational parameters for any scheme that attempts to reduce stocks.

The second stage

As scheduling adapts to the lower stock levels, the next stage is to improve the accuracy of forecasts. These are critical and each business will, very energetically, seek improvements in this activity. Differences between any forecast and the subsequent reality always have a measurable economic consequence, but lower overall stocks will magnify sensitivities to forecast fluctuations and impact on budgeted cash flow. Greater understanding of forecasting variations enables the companies to operate pragmatic introductory stock management arrangements that, hopefully, will become better defined and responsive. It is unlikely that these situations will surprise most shopfloor managers, as they will easily testify to the unpredictability of previous forecasts and the frequent short-term 'panic' measures undertaken to extricate their customer from a troubled situation.

The benefits for cooperation are shared. The customer may be surprised by the lax methodology used for forecasting, and the exaggerated pressures when the end of a trading period looms and the company budgets appear seriously out of reach! Production management will demand the constant availability of QC-validated supplies and any changes to supply procedures must have their tacit support. Such circumstances will promote the search to achieve better cash flow, reduce and, hopefully, eliminate discontinued stocks and create greater storage space. Suppliers will gain from greater certainty in organising their production and, in turn, obtaining their own supplies. In all collaborative programmes, JIT (just-in-time) et al., every operational level becomes more sensitive to their heightened responsibilities as the previous higher stock is steadily reduced. It is a most powerful statement and the changed attitudes should be encouraged to build the enthusiasm for subsequent development stages as the companies seek to determine the optimum operational stock levels.

The transferred advice of production requirements, normally through electronic software programs, provides the supplier with firm commitments for the immediate future and a provisional forecast beyond that period. The firm statement allows for no alteration and both parties agree the timescale. However, the forecast has an agreed variable factor to reflect changes in sales. The FMCG market is volatile and causes frequent adjustments to which packaging suppliers are most sensitive.

Both parties should acknowledge that the early trials of the system must have achievable targets; failure would endanger goodwill and allow cynics to disrupt or even cancel further progress. The tactics should be a progressive 'tightening' of objectives as experience dictates. Both parties will be conscious of the havoc caused by unexpected disruptions that would endanger the smooth logistics flow and will agree appropriate emergency procedures. Supply dislocation caused, for instance, by fires at the supplier's premises or unofficial strike action are examples of situations that should have well-rehearsed automatic responses.

The partners will expect variations between the forecasted volumes and reality so that stocks will be defined by *minimum* and *maximum* levels. The minimum quantity, regardless of their location, will consist of fully approved material that can be used directly. This reflects the customer's need for supply assurance. The maximum level gives the supplier some flexibility to smooth production schedules so that, if the supplier wishes to exceed this level it is a risk for them, because there is no obligation on the customer to accept the excess stock. The maximum stock defines the extent to which the customer confidently anticipates the existing business to be certain. The supplier may deem exceeding this level to be a worthwhile risk because of derived operational and economic benefits. Often there is little danger because the operational timescale is sufficiently short but the consequences of 'overstocking' must be clearly understood.

A concomitant is the transfer of stock management to the supplier for all material prior to the customer's production floor. This arrangement triggers several additional operational changes; it alters the method of payment for goods and passes the QC process into the hands of the supplier.

If the relationship extends to payment being 'triggered' by incorporation into the customer's product(s), the legal ownership of the stocks held in customer storage facilities should be agreed. Ownership becomes important in financially sensitive situations in case of bankruptcy of either party, stock damage or loss, etc.

All relevant process data should be openly exchanged between parties on the agreed timescale. On-line real data may be essential where customer storage capacity is very small in relationship to the production throughput, i.e. expressed in hours. Normal information will be weekly based on sales, historical production, adjusted forecasts, stock rejection levels, any market returns and stocks held in all supplying positions. If the inter-company business is progressing satisfactorily between several functional interfaces, the stocks to the 'front' of the customer's production area may become included within the supplier's remit. Responsibility for *all* stocks becomes accepted by the supplier and the process of maintaining adequate stocks on the customer's premises leads to increased frequency of deliveries that are often less than full loads – an interesting and unexpected development.

Guinness is good for you – a case study

Guinness is one of the world's leading brewers and markets the most famous stout – it is brewed in 48 countries, sold in more than 157 countries and 10 million glasses are drunk every day. The company has developed a real-time supply programme that demonstrates the tremendous gains achievable by companies with support from their downstream partners.

The combination of directly transmitted accurate information and efficient logistics has delivered the following benefits in less than three years commencing in April 1997:

- total elapsed time in the supply chain from 1,411 hours to 600 hours;

- planning cycle time from three weeks to less than seven days;

- finished goods stock of five weeks' sales down to one to two weeks' sales;

- inventory accuracy up to 99% from 88%;

- a 4% reduction in major component costs;

- excess warehouse costs of £100,000 eliminated;

- out-of-date stock costs down to £10,000 from £390,000 (!); and

- customer service up from 95% to 99%.

This is not a chance result and innumerable companies have matched this performance. It is an awesome improvement that challenges other brewers to compete.

CHAPTER 15

Supplier performance programmes

Introduction

Supplier performance programmes have been developed for a multiplicity of business reasons.

- They provide an objective assessment of supply efficiency and create a climate for further improvements.

- They involve other company functions to measure suppliers and influence the selection procedures.

- They support purchasing in their search for better commercial terms.

- Very importantly, they are accepted and used by suppliers to generate change programmes within their own companies.

The earliest programmes were simple and focused on key materials or services. Since then, their remit has widened considerably and now forms an ongoing assessment role. The programmes have an independent open measurement system that assesses suppliers' abilities to meet targets. The system details the requirements, primarily for internal corporate functions, and through statistical analysis measures the capability of suppliers to satisfy these agreed objectives.

Conferences to which suppliers are invited should introduce these programmes. Periodic reports are issued to identify and measure progress. Experience supports the steady improvement of suppliers, the rate of which lessens through time. It is important that the ongoing target remains credible and attainable; remote and wishful objectives can be demotivational.

The programme is, probably, the most important innovation in recent years; it has been responsible for tremendous changes in the perception of the buying function from other internal disciplines. The acceptance of independent measures has removed, for the cynics, the well-worn accusations that purchasing were selecting suppliers for the cost benefits – to reach the budget prices – with little or no regard to service. Supplier selection was, historically, seen as the sole remit of purchasing and, unless forceful representations were made, the choice could be heavily motivated by costs.

Today, however, a typical performance programme includes requirements submitted by the company functions that directly experience the efficacy of the suppliers. This is a sea change and is revolutionary. It represents the fullest internal collaboration. No longer can production managers complain, sometimes bitterly, about the bias of buying staff when purchasing decisions are influenced by the performance data that they have been involved in creating and measuring. It eases the transition into supplier selection whereby other functions, armed with the performance data, will support the collective decisions in allocating business to chosen suppliers.

Introducing these programmes has been extremely powerful. In designing the measures, purchasing has involved all disciplines whose operational responsibilities are impacted by suppliers. It may be, for example, a manufacturing unit awaiting timely supplies or marketing requiring new designs within a date-specific timeframe.

Constructing measures approved by other internal functions and explained to the supplier base prevents any subsequent debate as to the efficacy and transparency of the results.

Operational considerations

A company deciding to introduce a measurement system should sift the requirements of the various departments, reduce these to a short manageable list and determine the scale and time module to be used.

It is probable that the list of requirements will be longer than is practically effective and it is suggested that a minimal list begin the process.

There are several reasons for this. To introduce a new system with a limited list of easy-to-understand elements makes familiarisation smooth, it facilitates acceptance by suppliers and allows the actual performance levels to be 'ratcheted' upwards without distractions. The buyers, in principle, have the basics of an intelligent scheme to highlight those companies likely to support the trend towards closer cooperation and, in reverse, identifying those unable, or unwilling, to pursue these objectives. The periodic reviews will reveal the suppliers who are incapable of adjusting to the faster pace of modern logistics.

Primary values are delivery timing, acceptable quality, correct documentation and satisfactory transit packaging, and the length of each assessment period will depend on consultation with suppliers and customers. Sufficient delivery volumes to create sound statistical analysis are required. The measurement scale will rank performance and, in the situation of multiple suppliers, document their relative success. It is an opportunity for buyers to use the data to improve the total supply package! Continued poor (unacceptable) performance may automatically cause penalties – cash or goods – and may support the reallocation of business by favouring the better suppliers. This process is

---

undeniable and should be followed. The company will expect suppliers to become responsive to the measurement schemes. The benefits are shared as better service creates advantages for the customer and awards the more successful suppliers; the logic is clear and costs are reduced.

Every good idea should carry a health warning!

Within this simplified arrangement, it is highly likely that the analysts, lovers of detail and statistically obsessed, will attempt to divert the scheme into a myriad variety of checks, multiple performance measures and, worst of all, additional administration costs by spawning new job titles! Spurred on by the mistaken belief that computerised records are easy and cheap to create and maintain, there will be serious attempts to expand the measures, shorten the timescale for review and fragment the analysis into esoteric pieces. This is expensive, diversionary, time-wasting and, worst of all, boring. It loses impact. *Beware.*

Ignore these blandishments; complexity is the very antidote to a cheap, effective arrangement that achieves most objectives. It satisfies the internal functions clamouring for attention and an input into supplier selection, promotes educated supplier choice and raises the profile of purchasing in the corporate psyche.

It is conceivable that performances will improve to such a level that moving beyond is counter-productive. It may be unnecessary, too expensive to achieve or the differentiation disappears. The introduction of another measure should be considered as a replacement. The Japanese removed qualitative measures because the checking became meaningless once perfection had been reached! Change is healthy and retains interest and focus. Management attention wanders if nothing alters and purchasing should remain alert to the need for variation.

As a reflection of the pace of modern society, the time span within which companies bring products 'to market' has become a performance measure to include internal functions and the supplier(s). Launch projects are often complex using multifunctional support and, normally, are directed by a manager specifically appointed for the purpose. The line manager creates an agreed programme against the original launch plan, and allots various activities within it. The support of the supplier is crucial and will be measured. Clear briefing, regular checking through the programme and agreed solutions whenever alternative options are either desired or forced identify solid professional management. The coordination of the supplier's activities is a purchasing responsibility and should, therefore, be an internal measure. It is an assessment of their supplier selection abilities!

Purchasing interpretation

Supplier performances enable purchasing to extend their negotiations; the data collected is evidence for further advantages. The buyer is given the opportunity to change the supplier profile on the historical performances or on the 'ratcheted' future performance targets. As the customer's expectations increase, so does the fallout among suppliers. Carefully handled, the programme can facilitate supplier rationalisation, if required, from this independent assessment. It is easy to justify the increased allocation of business to the better performers in exchange for further commercial concessions.

The programme results form an integral part of all purchasing negotiations. Whenever supplier performances fall badly, there may be a case for expecting compensation in some chosen form because of the cost disadvantage experienced by the customer.

In contrast, it removes any lingering suggestions of personal bias of the buyer. It has become much harder to justify the removal of a supplier whose performance record is not the poorest within the sector.

There are many expressions of performance that are provided by the suppliers, or claims of the level at which customers may look to them for guaranteed action. Computer service companies delight in describing their service levels – 'we can reach North Wales within four hours of an emergency call' – but they lack any statement as to the consequences of failing to achieve these laudable guarantees. Under these circumstances, it is proper for the customer to have recourse to a system of defined penalties. Unwarranted claims should suffer some financial consequence for any failure. Ignoring failure is true failure.

Benchmarking

Beyond the immediate service measurements there remains, for selected suppliers, an assessment procedure that examines the effectiveness of their internal operations. This is a programme not exercised for general suppliers but for those key companies whose support benefits from collaborative activity.

Benchmarking suppliers allows judgements to be made against other industry competitors; the process is an integral part of establishing ongoing competitive edge. Both companies benefit and share the assessment parameters. It is extremely valuable when the supplier, although important, is small and unable to provide the resources for this project. It may be time-consuming and expensive, perhaps including hired consultants to perform the task. It is probable that consultants possess large databases from which the required assessments may be easily extracted. Their extensive clientele will provide sufficient data for this procedure to be speedy, but costly.

Benchmarking is not universally needed; the project should be focused upon defined elements that are critical in cost. Every cost refinement reinforces the relationship and fortifies each company's status in their individual market.

CHAPTER 16

Supply disruptions

The debate about reducing supply

Arranging the supplier portfolio to achieve optimum efficiency, including product cost, can be difficult. The choices may appear straightforward but satisfying contradictory internal requirements will need careful evaluation.

Supply security is a major factor because commercial damage can be instantaneous. Scrambling to repair the fault and obtain quick relief is hard and expensive. In 1997 Perrier Water discovered chemical contamination in the water source and retrieved millions of bottles returned from customers, supermarkets and supply warehouses. They embarked on a publicity campaign to reassure the public, lost sales to their mainstream competitors who seized their chance, and spent considerable monies correcting the production controls before advertising their return to market.

To accept the maximum number of suppliers to achieve the lowest prices – through the medium of determined and constant 'Dutch' auctions – and supply security – through multiple supply points – is a simple strategy to allow buyers to sleep soundly.

These factors have weighed against supplier rationalisation and the cost advantages of improved production planning and stock control. Any change in supply arrangement has been viewed as taking the company into uncertain and uncharted waters. The production managers do not want to wait nervously for deliveries of critical materials when internal stock levels reach zero! Nothing causes more anxiety and provokes heat and disorder. Defenders of maintaining the status quo are numerous so that disciples of change need patience, considerable persuasion based upon live examples of success and the understanding that progress is slow, painful but rewarding – ultimately!

In all its various forms, supply chain logistics have provided business with considerable benefits; stock management is shared, demand information is available faster and the purchased materials are near faultless. From the introduction of JIT, especially in the car industry, a leaner flow has emerged; we are astounded by the claims concerning complex arrangements that have created stockless assembly plants with component parts feeding into the process in a seamless fashion. The sophistication is much admired and demonstrates the amazing benefits derived from full collaboration. Long may this continue – but, deep in the jungle, do we hear faint murmurs of discontent?

From its inception, the supply chain concept has leant heavily on a smooth, serene industrial landscape with no disruptions in service. The acquiescence, willing or unwilling, of the workforce has been the major key to this advance. Any change to this fragile balance could cause serious problems. Buyers will be very sensitive to potential fractures as disruptions re-enter the industrial scene!

These examples illustrate the dangers attendant upon supply dislocations that can follow spontaneous or organised actions.

1. In 1997 Toyota halted production in Japan after a fire at a supplier, Aisin Seiki, which provided vital brake parts. 'The way in which a single factory fire has been able to bring Japan's largest car manufacturer to its knees has raised the question of whether the just-in-time, or *kanban*, manufacturing system pioneered by Toyota needs to be reviewed.' The company lost a full week's production before emergency supplies could be obtained. Events showed the risks of Toyota's great reliance on its network of *keiretsu*, or group, suppliers.

   Such problems had been highlighted in 1995 when an earthquake in western Japan cut off many suppliers. As a result, many car manufacturers conducted simulation tests of alternative actions in the event of a repetition. It focused attention on the risks of relying on one supplier for the majority of specific components.

2. In spring 1998, Saab, the Swedish automotive group, halted production at two factories after running out of essential components from strike-bound Danish supplying plants. A week-long national strike that affected Metallic, an engineering corporate, exhausted supplies of engine mountings of the Saab 95 and 93 saloons so that the press, body panel and paint shops were shut down. Saab warned that 4,250 employees would be forced to stop work and could be laid off within a week! *Saab also warned that many of its component suppliers would suffer following its decision to halt production.*

3. General Motors shut down all production facilities because of a strike. 'The strike is disrupting so-called "just-in-time" supply chains and now [June 1998] affects 220,000 workers! More than 9,000 workers protested against the decision to invest in low-cost production facilities in Mexico. Shortfalls have led to showrooms running out of stock so that TV and newspaper advertising has been suspended for the duration of the strike.'

   Salutary lessons that demand adjustments to the supply strategies.

4. Bajaj, an Indian motorbike manufacturer modelling itself on General Motors, 'cannot afford to rely on only one supplier for a particular part because its operations would be paralysed if that supplier's workers went on strike – a common occurrence in India's highly unionised manufacturing industry.'

Experimenting with new suppliers and systems requires considerable internal lobbying and preparation. The proposed alterations should be fully explained and concerns given careful consideration. Subject to majority approval the reduction of supplier sites will be accepted. While the workforce is supportive, or – more importantly – benign, this process of trimming supply points will allow 'doubting' factions to evaluate the changes and express their apprehension in an atmosphere of trust and confidence. Each change requires a clear expression, prior to implementation, of the commercial benefits and an objective measure of progress throughout.

The ultimate logic of this process is a single supplier using a single manufacturing point, which will, inevitably, cause the maximum unease. This position will need essential fail-safe measures over which the customer has the sole option of implementation. Depending on the complexity of the product and/or the supply chain, the customer may invoke an agreed option at any time, for example when there are disruptions, deemed serious by the customer, in the smooth product flow.

Any contract should define (a) the approved source of regular supply; (b) the alternative source in the event of a supply difficulty or rejected material; and (c) the alternative supplier, customer approved, from which product may be drawn, under circumstances of major disruption(s), without any contractual price penalty for the customer. Several internal functions will be expected to participate in this decision-making process. Without shared responsibility, the odds of achieving an acceptable solution is zero. This discussion should be managed and the options measured financially for their impact on corporate profitability.

Purchasing will be expected to agree the options with the existing supplier. It will include hard-fought negotiations because the latter will wish to protect their business base from competitive incursions. Given the natural uncertainty of materials availability, transport disruptions and labour attitudes, all parties will respect the logic but the supplier will want to retain total control over support operations. Regardless of the debate, friendly or otherwise, the decisions should be agreed and clearly recorded. Hopefully never to be used.

It is possible that the present supplier may, to exclude any potential competitor and at his own expense (!), construct a halfway stock cushion to give the most appropriate comfort for the client.

An interesting corollary to reducing supply stocking to minimum levels can be a commensurate adjustment in the payment terms. While this prevents the additional space created by JIT-style systems, it has the advantage of giving comfort in extremely stretched supply chains. This is the customer's choice but there is no shame in relying on extended credit as a partial sop to the no-stock proponents. Having the ability to press an insurance claim is no compensation for fulfilling customer's expectations. It is a matter of balance.

It is a matter of scale as well! In industries submitting themselves to lean supply arrangements, the pace at which a localised problem becomes widespread is magnified. There are several manifestations; one supplier failing to supply an integral component within an assembled unit creates ripple effects for each other supplier dependent upon the smooth production of the unit. Sales surges for one product generate supply dislocation throughout the chain; demand following media promotions may cause out-of-stock circumstances that suck product down the chain. This is often in response to exaggerated expressions of demand to prevent continuing supply constraints, and normality is returned very slowly and at some cost to all!

Depending on the pressure for storage capacities some consideration should be given to the option of 'extending' payment terms *and* continuing to hold stocks throughout the supply chain at levels that ensure availability. The preservation of 'full' stocks (and some!) may reassure those of fragile temperament and distrustful of smooth predictable material flows. While they may be accused of anachronistic attitudes, there may be value in merely adjusting payment terms to acknowledge the desire for lower stocks but without the clarity to devise an acceptable solution.

CHAPTER 17

Technical support

Introduction

Purchasing needs support from many quarters in the determined drive to obtain the best value performances. Any flexibility in the specification should be tested; the guardians of the specification will be challenged and enjoined to declare the limits within which purchasing may operate. Engineers, chemists, food technologists and architects may countenance alternative materials, sometimes on a like-for-like basis and sometimes on differing levels of performance.

In this debate, it is important to discover the options because the buying game is played on pitches defined by others. They are the referees and should prevent any trespass. The company purchases against their specifications and they remain the arbiters of corporate taste.

A commercial technician – Eureka!

To discover a technician who has a fundamental understanding of the purchasing remit is to find the Holy Grail. This person needs to be respected for their competence by supplier and customer. They should be absolutely abreast of the changes in public demands for quality assurance and retain a clear understanding of the company desire to maximise profits.

They do not fall off every tree *but* are precious *and* they may exist at the supplier – absolute gems who, stunningly, have little appreciation of their own value!

There must be an extensive debate to develop their interest in your objectives. Treasure these people and make them an integral part of the inter-company business team. They may be paid by your supplier and integrated within the joint development programme but they are an important element of your total resource capabilities.

Imagine this person being offered another job that removes their contribution from the partnership! A decision on their replacement becomes very important and you should expect to be consulted. Sharing staffing decisions for positions that impact upon the shared business should be seen as automatic. The relationship is totally absorbed with building a collective sense of camaraderie.

Most buyers seek the widest range of options possible. In markets where prices move in a relative manner and materials may be partially or fully interchangeable, the opportunity of reducing costs, by substitution, should be maximised. Buyers will be pushing the boundaries of acceptance outwards constantly and the technicians will arbitrate. They will provide a series of acceptable alternative materials that the company may use and a measurement system will be derived to compare alternatives and their impact on productivity levels and consumers. Bingo, the game is on!

Quality control – concentrated

Under normal business procedures, both supplier and customer perform similar quality control checks on the material supplied to confirm that the specification has been met. The supplier is responsible for approving the material and associated transport packing at the time of despatch. It is extremely important that goods and services are not damaged through inadequate protection while in transit. Modern packaging materials form an effective barrier and instances of goods being damaged in transit are becoming isolated. Most sophisticated logistics companies have very good secondary transit protective packaging standards to meet this need.

The modern emphasis on seamless supplies expects that products may be used immediately after receipt as soon as the transporting protection is removed. With leaner supply chains and lower stock levels, the potential for major disruption caused by such damage is easy to comprehend.

The customer has quality control personnel to validate that the goods conform to specification and the assessment should be performed at the earliest opportunity, ideally on delivery, so that rejected materials are not offloaded. The contractual terms may detail the timescale for rejection of submitted materials. A consequence of rejection is non-payment of the invoice and could involve claims for the costs, incurred by the customer, in handling the delivery.

It is not difficult to imagine the circumstances that precipitated the slogan of 'right first time' because it removes any element of unnecessary and costly administration. Customers, anxious about cash flow considerations, have used part-rejection as a tactic to delay all payments and perhaps encourage the supplier to add further incentives to the ongoing business.

The QC control process should establish that purchased products are totally suitable for processing. This, however, is an expression of hope rather than expectation because the specification is not sufficiently comprehensive to exclude equipment variability that may cause complications. Obviously it is critical that operational functions continue to perform their tasks without any interruptions. The QC process is, therefore, the acceptance, by the buying company, of the products. It becomes more difficult, often impossible, to recover any costs or materials if the purchased goods fail to perform beyond this initial check.

The efficacy of existing QC controls has been questioned, especially in industries where the procedure cannot account for more than a percentage of the supplied volumes. With large deliveries of the same product it is normal practice for the customer to sample the delivery. The sample proportion is calculated to be statistically sound to ensure the whole delivery is acceptable.

It is easy to understand this procedure being transferred to the supplier because it allows any consequent failure to be directly attributable to the supplier and all cost consequences of the failure, measured assiduously by corporate auditors, may be recovered. The current vogue for lean corporate structures encourages this transfer of responsibilities.

To contemplate this operational shift suggests that the supply relationship has progressed satisfactorily and the supplier has a full understanding of the customer's operational needs. The purpose and processes to which the purchased product will be subjected should be fully understood, which requires the customer to provide a practical demonstration. This allows a closer review of the process equipment foibles and variations that may not have been included in the ongoing statements of practice. The supplier will have the opportunity of detailing these variations and, probably, stretching the product specification as a consequence.

Many informal adjustments to procedures exist that 'manage' to utilise product variations without ever being brought to the attention of purchasing management. Shopfloor operatives are adept at 'fiddling' machines to accept packaging materials and factory managers may continue sublimely ignorant of the fact! However, the operational examination should force these nuances to be examined, defined and included in the new procedures and specifications. It exposes adjustments that have, historically, not been included in the inter-company agreement. All these activities provide an infinitely better understanding of the actual practices that have an impact upon the finished products.

The drive for lean slim business structures supports a single quality control process. The companies will agree an alternative QC procedure that requires either technical function to complete an exhaustive checking process of the material so that it may be directly processed. The automotive industry, for example, has lean supply arrangements that enjoy zero stocks held at the receiving production plant as component parts are delivered to production lines just 15 minutes ahead of their incorporation into a vehicle. Much lauded as an example of close coordination between supplier and customer, this illustrates the effectiveness of QC control performed by the supplier.

Although this change has dramatically improved supply chain efficiencies, the global milk industry has experienced the inherent skill by which Tetrapak has created filling machines that work optimally with their own packaging. In principle, other packaging formats should match the performance of Tetrapak cartons but there remains slight deficiencies that favour the combination – and it needs little imagination to hear the complaints when the use of third-party packaging causes problems. A challenge for buying negotiators!

In the revised QC checking procedure exercised by the supplier, it is clear that stocks, prior to the customer's process, are subject to these controls. It links with the legal ownership of products (see elsewhere) and moves the relationship forward to the reorganised payment arrangements.

The reduction in internal QC management may either be absorbed in lower corporate overheads or result in freeing personnel time for other technical control work that could include supplier visits. This exchange of information and opinions eases the inter-company progress. Improved understanding of operational constraints and opportunities will add to the mutual benefit process. In circumstances where supplier and customer are significantly different, the 'stronger' partner may be able to facilitate progress for the other. Exchanging ideas is a fertile process!

The regular publication of all QC checks is vital; it forms a measure of supplier performance and provides an incentive for further improvement. Every company needs to be associated with efficient suppliers and confirmation of their standing and progress is essential to build confidence. This process provides objective and undisputed details of performance. It strips away the bland ongoing hope and expectation that improvements are shortly to be realised. QC reporting is involved in assessing overall supplier performances through agreed measures. The relative standing of the supplier base supports purchasing tactics in reallocating customer business; it is the natural process of rewarding those who continue to outperform the market.

Specifications – challenging the status quo

Buyers should consistently challenge the existing business, especially for the quality of purchased goods and services. Can there be any variation that the company would accept and which would produce additional benefits, either in monetary terms or service levels?

Buyers should be required to source requirements against an approved specification, which will usually be produced in collaboration with suppliers. The easiest example is of market standard goods with a generic specification. Most materials fit this arrangement but, in more complex circumstances, there will be a unique material which is needed by the customer and for which the technical staff from supplier and customer have specifically designed an individual specification. Occasionally the customer will have produced the specification alone and the supplier is acting as a subcontractor.

To maintain commercial sharpness, the specification should reflect the most appropriate component. While the majority of alternatives will involve lowering the specification, there remain considerable options for higher specified products whose use extends substantially beyond the existing specification. The objective is to realise better unit costs for the end product. Technicians, from supplier and customer, have an important role to discharge in the search for materials matching, equalling or, hopefully, beating the competition. Higher concentrated materials use smaller storage space, for example. In this search, the technical personnel are key supporters, particularly from the supplying company. Extending business is the result and the combined functions should regularly monitor progress towards this goal.

CHAPTER 18

Supply partnerships – are they flawed?

Introduction

Supply partnerships are the current fashion and, predictably, create slavish unthinking mimicry. Very often managers can be drawn into self-delusion by the imagined gains to be harvested. Every chief executive – pressed by the critical examination of shareholders – grasps thankfully at the instant benefits that will surely flow as the chosen supplier becomes responsible for the stock-holding process that his own company has failed to manage effectively in the past. Here comes a white knight able to introduce good operational management by reducing stock-holding levels – to free up additional warehouse space at the client's premises and cut the cash mountain wrapped up in the pre-production stocks – under the guise of gaining manufacturing programme benefits. It seems like Christmas – and short-term gains blot out any future potential hazards.

Buying has a constant variety that dictates different tactics for each material/service to achieve the most advantageous arrangement for the company. There needs to be irrefutable reasons for entering any partnership agreement. Is there a commercial advantage? Does the chief executive really understand? Is it the answer to pressure for short-term gains?

Knee-jerk reactions drive the process resolutely forward as surely as lemmings off a cliff.

Because partnerships imply a longer-than-normal relationship, the debate should be exhaustive. (a) It must understand the need for changing the status quo – if there is a problem, are there other options available to solve the issue? (b) In particular, it must be conversant with the company strategy and have participated in its formulation – to select suppliers without this knowledge is inviting catastrophes to strike the ignorant. Every buyer knows the chagrin of discovering, too late, the new product formulated by New Product Development with material and supplier already selected, along with the machine that the company engineers openly prefer that concedes total negotiation advantages to the supplier. (c) The future company strategy can only be shared with the supplier when safeguards that have legal teeth are in place; gone are the days, unfortunately, of assumed trust. The informal grapevine works effectively with the chauffeur, secretary and post-boy being infallible sources of news. (d) Of critical importance is the expectation of future benefits that will continue beyond 'jam today and to hell with tomorrow'. (e) An understanding is required of the release mechanisms (divorce) that may be needed. (f) The company reveals longer and firmer production requirements. (g) Operating control is transferred. (h) Internal knowledge of the company procedures and personnel is exposed.

Most important, however, are the market reactions. Other potential suppliers react predictably; no quotes, stupidly expensive quotes and destructively damaging undercutting quotes. Is benchmarking of any value? The 'free' market information – that industry flow of gossip – dries up and the buyer is subject to selective information from their chosen partner. The selected supplier certainly benefits from customer loyalty for an attractively long period, greater production flexibility, more 'inside' information, fewer challenges from competitors and, perhaps, cost-plus costing. The last is a 'catchall' for every sin that the supplier commits and for which the unwitting customer pays.

So – it could be a disaster! Away goes competitive advantage – what negotiation? Away goes strategic planning – but the supplier committed people, time and equipment to your plans, which have now been withdrawn, so away goes manufacturing know-how, especially the weaknesses. Away goes intellectual property and away goes the purchasing function. Once the agreement is completed, there is no need, is there?

Supplier partnerships are the Devil's creation – get it right and there are stunning gains, but get it wrong and the knacker's yard beckons. Every energetic supplier will be anxious to lock in their customers to this comforting long-term relationship which, handled correctly, can be a licence to print money.

The subject demands total concentration and clear focus. Caveat emptor!

Breaking up is hard to do – and you'd better believe it! The early hopes and aspirations turn to dust as the relationship hits choppy seas and sinks with acrimony, leaving both partners facing commercial problems. With divorce commonplace nowadays there is no justification for ignoring the possibility of separation before beginning a supply partnership. Too often companies have launched themselves forward together without knowing how to manage potential separation.

Recriminations are very expensive and pre-marital contracts, despite appearing cynical and lacking rosy-cheeked optimism, must assure the partners of their continuing commercial independence and viability. How do you handle your partner's adulterous activity with an uncomfortable competitor of yours? Is there an engagement period before 'launching' a fully integrated relationship? What protection can be established when your partner experiences a change in control? If your partner becomes too assertive and creates impending economic doom, can you run away? Well-reasoned agreements, supported by commercial law, are essential prerequisites for confident partnerships. Everything must be based on compatibility and a shared vision of the future. *Stepping out without a supportive framework is commercial stupidity.*

So how do you prepare? Very, very carefully!

Most partnerships spring from recognising that another company has been especially attentive to your needs and that commercial benefits can be unlocked by reciprocating. Partners begin the natural (informal) sharing process that encourages the prospect of closer combined activities. Dispassionate evaluation by the purchasing function will assess the options in building a formal partnership. Much has been written about the selection process but an essential element is determining the courtship period (the 'shakedown' in agreeing the operating basis for the partnership) within which timescale the participants may decide to stop. Shotgun marriages leave one partner unenthusiastic and a potential deserter. An unbalanced relationship is not excluded as long as the exchanges are proactive.

Job descriptions for everyone!

Each company must clarify the need for partnership in achieving their strategic targets; considerable work in selecting the 'right' partner should involve every function that will be directly involved in the relationship. Regardless of the initial sponsorship, the responsibility for overseeing the smooth implementation and maintenance must be held by purchasing. Their historical knowledge of potential suitors and understanding of internal objectives gives them an unrivalled advantage. Having collected a communal agreement to proceed and establish the relationship on a formal basis it is important to define the functional responsibilities within each company; indistinct and blurred 'job descriptions' can lead to uncomfortable claims and muddle.

Regular health checks

Repeated reviews to examine progress, resolve troubles and reaffirm continuing and progressive integration will form the basic cement. No relationship is ever static and moving forward is the desired option. Backing out should be the last resort and made commercially very difficult. Changed company ownership may bring about a volte-face and a determination to abandon many previous partnerships almost regardless of the economic consequences on the other partner. If there is none, except a staged apology, the rudderless player will have nothing of consolation or comfort.

Get out option

Escape clauses are vital to ensure that unlocking the relationship is painless. To discover, halfway through a very expensive shared R & D project destined to gain market advantage, that your partner lacks any further funding capabilities is totally destructive. Scrabbling to source alternative productive capacity while the competition moved ahead and launched earlier damaged a major company so much that market share suffered permanently!

Life is flawed and any entirely smooth relationship deserves suspicion; to resolve family squabbles – despite mediation efforts – may require the heavy-handed drive from 'above' to focus attention upon the objectives. Within each review period there will be agreed exchanges between partners that bring corporations closer. These should illustrate increasing confidence and every stage should be protected by the formal acceptance of data and confidential information and further commercial benefits for the providing company. Each player needs to feel, see and hear the moving linkage yielding measurable gains. Neither partner can continue to 'talk up' the benefits without seeing tangible evidence. Each arrangement is unique but all share the ambition to deliver gains, ideally for all! Those gains are quantifiable and continuous so that each period of the relationship should see improvements given to each partner. Close integration must bring greater efficiencies in its wake. This is an essential measure of progress together and, if missing, forces reassessment. To err, within reason, at the first review may be forgivable but to miss agreed targets at the second should send warning signals to the partner. 'Blue skies' visioning is rejected and reality must tinge every projection.

Cash penalties

The expectations of benefits available during the partnership period should be openly discussed so that separation will carry penalties. An appraisal of missed opportunities should be made and the 'leaving' partner should recognise the loss that the innocent party will incur. This may be hardheaded, but the commercial contribution from successful partnerships is adequate justification. It focuses attention immediately and precludes irresponsible pretence. Modern business has a multitude of 'charter' arrangements that encourage penalties for inadequate performance and partnership should be viewed in the same light. For instance, two clients, linked by partnership, agreed to adjust transfer pricing between each review as an acknowledgement of the implicit penalties and used this salutary experience to improve their individual internal performance.

Personal attention

The partnership has an 'unspoken' recognition that each participant, for sound commercial reasons, will not pursue relationships with natural market competitors. There are many practical reasons that become more persuasive as the integration develops. Every effort must be made to ensure that the exchange of very sensitive commercial information cannot be leaked. What is wrong with open debates about companies with whom each partner is considering doing business and gaining the approval of the other? The potential trading option has to be directly related to the supply arrangement and any rejection must be fully justified. Future capital planning is drawn into discussion as servicing most developments requires closely integrated arrangements. Having sufficient money to fund a partner's market aspirations would be a pre-requisite for any proactive partnership. Relationships often begin in an area of serious technical development, e.g. a new process, machinery, with an associated cash expense.

Tell-tale signs (lipstick on the collar!)

What will be the clues to impending separation as familiarity develops boredom and slipshod attitudes and more attractive propositions emerge elsewhere? Watch for missed deadlines, sending along replacements to meetings, blaming others, weakening commitment – especially for financial investment – and innocent/deliberate blurring of focus. The purchasing staff should 'mother' the players back together; each function has a responsibility to advise on relationships with their counterparts.

How to separate painlessly

Hopefully the earlier comments will minimise the need to split but if it is unavoidable, do it *early*! Really confidential information is exchanged as the relationship develops and any that is perceived as critical should be retained in an isolated neutral position with controlled access granted to the other partner. Each review is an opportunity to confirm the collective desire to progress. If not, the separation should proceed through the contractual period. Consulting experience indicates that a 'live' issue is the misunderstanding that exists between purchasing functions. The lean, mean environment is bringing purchasing performances constantly to CEOs, so it is vital that the separate groups cohabit positively and clearly recognise the opportunities and constraints in each other's markets. Shared information makes for better relationships. Two recent examples will suffice to emphasise the importance of clear responsibilities: (1) a supplier took raw material contracts, on behalf of their client, well beyond the decoupling period and – *yes* – the market moved against the cover position! (2) one client fervently believed that the partner's purchasing staff were offloading poor buying decisions on to them – a captive customer! The most difficult position is new product development for which each party has detailed information, may have built prototypes and understood the intended marketing strategy; the closer sharing of corporate plans concedes advantages that are impossible to hold. Just a little faith and crossed fingers.

Love and hate are mirror images

Total guarantees don't exist but dissolving the relationship should always be the reverse of building the agreement. Avoiding broken glass and shattered dreams is the stuff of practical management. Simple checks and regular escape options ensure sanity because prevention is always better than cure.

> 'Oh, I say, could you fold up your supplier pitch on the park and go now – not tomorrow, *now*! We've had enough and we have no responsibility towards you at all. *What cost*? See you in court.'

CHAPTER 19

Cash flow: the company
bloodstream

Simple processes yield further advantages and it pays to concentrate!

Introduction

The alternative methods of paying for goods and services contain sufficient options to enhance the purchasing performance. To hold money in the company bank account earning interest is important and, crucially, the higher the rate of interest, the greater this benefit becomes. Thirty per cent of businesses admit to using late payment as a source of credit and this tactic forms part of the corporate policy. Many companies issue guidelines that detail invoice terms and the corresponding company terms; a supplier may request payment in 30 days from receipt of invoice, but the customer's formal direction is at the end of the month following receipt! Experience suggests that suppliers are conscious of these differences and will try to adjust other elements of the business in an attempt to recover.

A most successful modern example is that of supermarkets whose stock management and the excellent payment terms negotiated with their suppliers allow them to supervise a totally positive cash flow scenario, circumstances that they have used to fund their business expansion.

Cash flow is critical to every company, especially those moving through the stages of early growth, but many established firms suffer considerable cash pressure and seek relief by slowing payments. In 2000, MG Rover, a loss-making British carmaker, advised suppliers that, unilaterally, it was to change from 60-day payment terms to 90 days, in an effort to improve their financial state! Somerfield, a second-division UK supermarket group, who were facing a painful profits shortfall in the same year, introduced a retrospective price reduction for goods that had already been sold! The payments were to inflate profits on the immediate past trading period. The action was an exercise of raw power that could probably remove the weaker suppliers.

There are many amusing anecdotes detailing the extremes that companies will reach in seeking payment of overdue debts. Most tactics involve an element of creating public embarrassment and shame in an effort to extract payment. Of course, debts from a single transaction that is unlikely to be repeated can be attacked in this manner but should the relationship contain any vestige of continuing business, this process is certainly going to foreclose such prospects speedily.

Much heat has been generated by concern about the iniquitous manner in which larger customers pay small businesses. Payments made beyond the timescale recorded on invoices have been universally applied and cause cash pressures for the suppliers. Formal attempts to counteract these financial disadvantages risk automatic court penalties exercised in favour of the suppliers. The prospects of this politically inspired procedure generating positive rewards are zero! It takes little to imagine the brief discussions between customers and suppliers. Modern research finds that an overwhelming majority of small business are hostile to such an approach, which they believed would actually be used against them by their larger customers.

And what has this to do with buying? Each company requires clear guidance, to be provided by the finance department, as to the manner in which payments are made, and purchasing should negotiate the terms with suppliers. It should be viewed as an integral element of the total cost of the goods and services provided. Purchasing should agree with financial managers all payment terms prior to implementation.

These arrangements should be managed and negotiated by the buying team. It has a widespread impact on company financing requirements, cash flows and the cost of every purchase. While the management of corporate money is the remit of the finance function, there is a considerable element that can be influenced by the buyers.

The existing practice should be understood and discussed. If there are several procedures to approve purchases because of multiple sites or buyers, it is probable that the payment arrangements will differ. It may be that computerised cheque issues do not permit unique terms for a specific supplier to be accepted; the company may not wish to electronically transmit payments. There are innumerable considerations for which finance has management responsibility.

Strategic considerations

Purchasing is directly involved in negotiating payment arrangements because of the cost implications. It is another element of the complete cost of goods that is capable of being influenced by buyers. The negotiating remit allows them to capture additional benefits; the tactic is to protect company cash flows.

Why should I give away company money until the latest possible moment? And, if I do, what can I receive for the concession?

Money given to the supplier is no longer able to promote and build the company because it is dispensed to maintain the status quo. It is therefore incumbent upon the buyer to organise the optimal payment terms in the effort to meet several, and often conflicting, objectives.

There is well-merited concern that the process involves a total disregard for terms included in the suppliers' invoice documentation. Almost every document exchanged between companies contains individually unique terms not recognised, in practice, by the other party. The situation is handled pragmatically and the muddle continues. Accounts departments the world over pay invoices according to a format that measures the importance of the supplier and their associated terms.

It seems inevitable that, today, the most important objective is to secure written terms that are acceptable to both parties and will stand the close attention of the law. The buyer will ensure that the company is accepting compliance with the supplier and forestall any public accusation of unfair practice and, probably more importantly, ease the business relationship with suppliers.

The angry telephone calls seeking payments that, rightly, should have been made several days before can become a distant memory.

However, any payments on the timescale requested by the supplier should enjoy attractive terms for that compliance.

Both parties should commence their trading relationship with a clear understanding about payment timing and procedures. If the business is to become important to the parties, there should be no doubt as to the agreed terms.

Staged payments that are dependent upon the satisfactory completion of the contractors' agreed actions should retain sufficient pressure to ensure total compliance. It is a necessary tactic and should be recognised for its tenuous value; there is little salvation in smugly holding some monies for a project that is in 'free-fall'. Retained money can be used to arrange alternative solutions but the customer as much as the supplier will view it as a failure. Every management sinew should be strained to ensure careful completion and project progress must therefore be closely monitored.

Currency risk management

Most companies have, directly or indirectly, imported purchases that consequently contain an element of exchange rate exposure. This may be significant and deserving of attention. Requesting suppliers to quote in the currency of the customer may be easy but the process of translating the price could mask some protective assessments to increase the cost.

Attempting to forecast exchange rate movements successfully is impossible and the province of madmen; of course, at times there may be an inequality, universally recognised, that requires correction but the pace, timing and extent of the correction may not be equally predictable. Some British companies have, based upon advice or the subjective judgement of their finance director, suffered such horrendous losses that they have featured in their annual report. British Aerospace 'waved goodbye' to £146 million as subjective judgements 'got it wrong'! The steady acceptance of the euro will remove these variables for business inside the EU but the US dollar continues to be the pre-eminent currency for global trade. Its influence will continue for those trading beyond the EU confines, so an independent automated hedging system is essential for protection and certainty of costs. The administration of this mechanistic scheme is the responsibility of the finance department. A good management system will allow the company another opportunity of gaining additional advantages against competition. It cannot be ignored!

Some multinationals 'balance' their currency debts and earning against each other; if purchases are made in US dollars and a subsidiary is trading profitably in Brazil, these are balanced against each other to result in a reduced exposure. The hedge programme should, however, be viewed as a doubled opportunity to gain further advantages by 'defending' exchange rates in both currencies. The market schemes are sufficiently sophisticated for most company exposures to be confidently protected against major deviations.

How to pay

The multiplicity of payment options make this process very important; it takes no time to imagine the cost of money when interest rates move into double digit levels.

There are several important tactics for consideration.

1. During a period of low interest rates, the payment timing is less important, extending the term is of little value and the cost penalty is minimal. It is therefore very important to agree a long period of payment because any subsequent rise in interest levels will create advantages.

2. Conversely, discount for earlier payments are options to be negotiated whenever interest rates are high because the supplier will provide 'useful' discounts for the practice. As rates decline the advantage is created in a converse manner.

3. The methods of payment are debatable. Telegraphic transfer, second class post, bank cheques, etc. provide the buyer with several options that should provide better terms for services and goods. It is nonsense to concede this decision to financial functionaries. It is, however, important to submit the more indirect options that are devised for their opinion; there is no value in ignoring their advice.

The results of these options will, inevitably, be recorded differently and show either that cash flow has improved – a financial plus – or that goods and services are cheaper – a buying benefit to be transferred to other active functions. This may become a political process *but* it is very important not to lose it as a real opportunity.

Many companies find that these opportunities are 'lost' between different buying functions through negligence and ignorance. The level of cooperation is crucial to giving the company a continuing edge against competition. In extraordinarily contested markets the payments terms will assume considerable importance.

CHAPTER 20

Veto responsibility – the people issue

The most extreme illustration of inter-company cooperation is the ability of either party to directly influence the internal decision-making procedures of the other, particularly for personnel appointments that have an inordinate impact upon the shared business. Such situations are too complex to occur in the acclimatisation and mutual testing of the early formative stages of the relationship.

It represents a mature relationship in which key business roles, performed in the partner company, are recognised for their exceptional influence on the ongoing and future business activities. The interface between parties will have developed very extensively for these circumstances to be contemplated; misplaced enthusiastic attempts to 'force the pace' may endanger progress. As companies adjust to their closer ties, people become a live issue. Among the functions that comprise the corporate interface, this factor has the most sensitive impact upon the nature of the relationship.

As both companies build understanding together they will recognise the key jobs in each partner – and hold views as to the current capabilities of the present jobholders! Insensitive managers whose attitudes or capabilities obstruct progress endanger many inter-company relationships; they impede the smooth discharge of responsibilities. Aside from the cultural differences between companies the need to change attitudes rests upon the flexibility of managers and their ability to communicate to their staff.

To create a supportive mindset is essential. A reasoned explanation defining the benefits, including disadvantages in operating procedures, is essential to obtaining support and understanding. To assume compliance is a speedy move towards hellfire and damnation!

Depending on the industry, there will be different functions that possess inordinate influence. Within FMCG (fast moving consumer goods) businesses, with the emphasis upon speedy responses, there will be considerable emphasis upon the supplier's production flexibility and the customer, therefore, will be keenly sensitive to the relationship between the planning and logistics managers. For engineering companies, on the other hand, quality control approval of all distributed products may be perceived as the key factor. Examine a packaging supplier and it becomes clear that quality control and production managers hold the key to providing a smooth fault-free supply for the further processes at their customers.

As commercial imperatives move business into a greater level of inter-dependence, and relationships ebb and flow, the nature of personal contacts is significant. As managers display their attitudes towards closer working procedures, their extra-functional capabilities may help the trading partner towards an appreciation of their worth. The influence of specific managers cannot be understated because they will have a direct impact on corporate profitability. It is, therefore, important to recognise those external managers who have the ability to change business health, perhaps to a stronger extent than internal employees!

For example, the commercial understanding of technical staff may elevate them in the eyes of a customer beyond colleagues who possess superior 'pure' technical knowledge. Solving a problem may, not unexpectedly, present a range of options that increases effectiveness with an additional cost, but identifying the preferred viable choice needs an appreciation of the commercial parameters. The ability to cross functional boundaries is an asset. Understanding the customer's priorities is invaluable and translating that knowledge into the internal support programmes is a key facility.

An Australian packaging company focusing on low-cost manufacturing of market quality plastic trays, had, in the spirit of lean staffing, forsaken technical development and filled the position with a manager competent to maintain support for the existing products only. Future planning was, by default, performed by competitors and the company relied upon their cost advantage to replicate any product innovation that appeared successful. A major client, wishing to develop the business from the attractively low price structure, was faced with this obstacle to progress and eventually demanded the recruitment of a manager to fill the development role. In the first year of the arrangement, the additional staffing cost was included within the product invoices. Holding on to the price advantage was an absolute priority and the premium demanded by the employment of a competent development manager deemed to be worth paying.

So, beyond corporate confines, there exist positions that can have an exaggerated influence. Is it, therefore, any surprise that personnel filling these key functions should be very important to the customer? Every communication channel between companies reflects corporate attitudes and personnel should discharge their additional responsibilities with care.

While establishing the new trading relationship will involve existing managers as 'link' players, should a vacancy arise it will provide an opportunity for the business partner to comment upon and approve candidates to succeed within those jobs. If inter-company relationships depend upon this being non-confrontational, for example, it is appropriate for prior notification of job changes, including the proposed personnel, to be offered to the customer for comment.

The manifestation of a veto process that empowers an important customer adds, sometimes uncomfortably, to the shared responsi-bility.

Unusual though this approach may appear, it illustrates critical key factors that separate those companies using partnerships from the alternative tactic of 'bullying' suppliers into continued submission. Every supply relationship needs outgoing positive and collaborative styles to succeed.

POSTSCRIPT

Managing external suppliers is crucial; they are the mirror image of the customers and equally special. Building a relationship that transcends the normal commercial demands and shares the vision is the most acceptable.

This book is about the relationships that are promoted, nurtured and established by the buying staff who form the human interface to filter, translate and manage communications while, simultaneously, seeking out opportunities for further gains.

Constructing supply partnerships is dramatic because of the pervasive internal consequences that flow from change, either in the manner of trading with an existing supplier or, more obviously, with a new supplier. It is the greatest challenge for purchasing and needs vision to anticipate the future and what arrangements are needed to satisfy the requirements of the company strategies. Strong personalities may, single-handedly, achieve it but the collective confidence generated by sensitive, and sensible, management is indispensable. The presence of internal support and appreciation of the buying contribution are key factors.

Every buyer should understand their influence – and responsibilities; persuading reticent and implacable internal colleagues to allow a potential supplier to submit products as substitutes for the existing arrangements can be exhausting. Breaking into an efficient flow with trials of other materials may be very costly – lost production through changeovers, for example.

To have confidence in any untried source demands sound business logic and steely resolve. Buying management must detail the perceived benefits to influence their colleagues so that every trial can be measured objectively. Well-managed and successful introductions will impress and raise the status of buying.

Convincing managers to buy into the vision of a better future is very tough. It is, naturally, easier to promote change if the existing arrangements are troublesome. Everybody wants to remove the problem – and fast!

Purchasing is charged with obtaining dependable supplies from attuned sources at competitive prices so that altering any existing arrangement shows the restless urge to seek further improvements.

All markets have new entrants and massive care is needed to sift out the most attractive, if there are such, alternatives for further evaluation. Internal functions need to pore over the potential supply source and the procedure entails constant stress. In today's pressurised world the competitive edge is sufficiently honed for each buyer to take every precaution before proposing a change to the status quo. But the prize just might be outstanding.

The constant search for the most fertile relationship keeps buying staff responding to almost every caller 'off the streets'. The dream of turning up the equivalent of the 'crock of gold' is undimmed. Adventure continues to be attractive and enticing.

In companies that demonstrate nervous caution, buyers retreat into an understandable defensive stance that yields little and confines their performance to a dull repetitive measurement based only on invoiced costs. It is an element in the risk-averse attitudes that prevent full development of a supply partnership and allow the purchasing role to slump into an unedifying rut in which they stay unnoticed, unloved and, often, unwanted – the lost little boy on the boundary edge incapable of catching the captain's eye and committed to a lifetime of wondering about his isolation.

The commercial world always contains contrasting examples of success that reflect operating choices. The battering ram of aggressive uncomplicated buying may yield results and rewards as long as markets possess one weak seller and as long as supply systems do not encounter shortages. There is no real need for any sophisticated knowledge other than the advantages of the severe psychological bruising of salesmen. It matters little if partnership benefits can be created whilst weakness continues to give up acceptable invoiced prices.

The contention in this book is that greater, wider and longer-lasting benefits can be drawn forth with both supplier and customer sharing gains from their partnership. There is a range of activities beyond the price negotiations that translate into commercial gains. It requires imagination and wit to test the willingness of everyone to unlock those nuggets – and the perseverance of Job. There is nothing that slog and sheer hard work cannot yield. Readers should be encouraged to 'dream the dream' and take their colleagues along the path towards enlightened partnerships.